THANK GOD FOR DEPRESSION

Published by Inner Sky Books

Printed in the United States
ISBN (paperback): 979-8-9873422-0-6
ISBN (ebook): 979-8-9873422-1-3

THANK GOD FOR DEPRESSION

Make Depression the Best Thing to Ever Happen to You

Kyle Nicolaides

TABLE OF CONTENTS

Disclaimer.. i

Introduction 1

Chapter 1: A New Perspective..5
            A Bush, Ayahuasca, and a Whole New World

Chapter 2: First Steps... 27
            The Do's of Depression

Chapter 3: Depression 101... 59
            Depression for Dummies

Chapter 4: Self-Care 85
            Wisdom from a Haunted House

Chapter 5: How to Talk About Your Depression 121
            Conversations on Sasquatch

Chapter 6: Thoughts... 147
            A Yoga Teacher Training Gone Horribly Wrong

Chapter 7: Presence.. 169
            Just Eat the Mushrooms, Babe

Chapter 8: Identity.. 193
            Of Gods and Karens

Chapter 9: Living in Alignment 213
            A Life Inventory

Chapter 10: Suicide 237
            One Day Soon but Not Now

Chapter 11: Consciousness... 249
            A Mystical Conclusion

Acknowledgments 261

Recommended Reading 267

About the Author 269

DISCLAIMER

This book includes a lot of stories from my days in a rock band and misadventures with psychedelic plant medicine. The stories in this book are for interest only.

Plant medicine is illegal in the United States (and so should getting together with your dipshit friends to start a rock band and the gallivanting that ensues), and I can't suggest or recommend the use of plant medicine to anyone reading this. Any application of those practices is at the reader's own risk, and the author and publisher disclaim any liability arising directly or indirectly from them.

Furthermore, the information presented is the author's opinion and does not constitute any professional mental health, health, or medical advice. The content of this book is for informational purposes only and is not intended to diagnose, treat, cure, or prevent any condition or disease.

Please seek advice from your healthcare provider for your personal health concerns prior to taking healthcare advice from this book.

Mom and Dad, this book is for you.
Thank you for everything. I love you so much.

INTRODUCTION

If you're reading this, I'm sorry.

I'm sorry because, if you're reading this, I can safely assume that depression has been donkey-kicking your life. Living with depression is an existence scary enough to make any Stephen King novel seem like an episode of the Teletubbies. I would not wish it upon anyone. I get it. I was depressed for over ten years of my life.

I'm as shocked as anyone to be writing this introduction because this book was never supposed to exist. This is because I never thought for a second that I would ever get out of the depression I was in.

Then I found unexpected healing in a way that was so miraculous and mystical that it gave meaning and purpose to the entire span of my depression. Now I'm here with a message—if I can find healing and light, anyone can. So this book was born.

I'm an artist by trade, a songwriter and musician. I believe artists are alchemists. We alchemize our own suffering into light, belonging, and healing for other people. My purpose in life and on this planet is to bring light to people, and this book is the best way I know how to do it. While I never had "author of a self-help book on mental health" on my life bingo card, here we are.

This is the book I wish I would have had at twenty because I know all the knowledge in here would have saved me a decade of my life. I joke that I put my ten thousand hours into depression so you don't have to. But one of my biggest inspirations in writing this book was the question, what if my ten years of depression could be your five months because of this book?

This book is everything I've learned in my ten-year journey with depression. This book is about alchemy. It teaches you how to turn depression from a terrorist into a teacher and make it the biggest gift you've ever received. I argue that consciousness and intelligence exist within depression, and there's a reason it's in your life. I teach you how to find light, purpose, and meaning on your mental health journey. This book is about how to live a better, happier, more fulfilling, and healthier life because of your depression.

In the pages ahead, I share every single bit of wisdom that helped me, offered relief, and brought me light on my mental health path. Believe me, I have tried everything on this plane and the astral planes to find a way through. I put everything I know in this book and want to share it all with you. It's a handbook for how to step out of the darkness and into the light.

Together, we'll look at depression through the different lenses of spirituality, consciousness, authentic living, identity, self-care, thoughts, presence, belief systems, and trauma and learn how they relate to your depression.

When I was depressed, I was bummed at the lack of resources offered by people who actually understood what I was going through. That's why I wrote this book.

The message of this book is a formerly depressed person saying to another depressed person, "Here's how to find purpose, meaning, and healing on your mental health journey. I did it, and you can too."

My overwhelming message is that there is hope for you. I spent my twenties in a self-sabotaging blackout, blindly crashing into not one but all of the mistakes, and despite all that, I managed to find redemption, meaning, light, and healing. So can you. You can and will get out of this. If one person is capable of healing, all people are, and all people deserve it. You deserve to be happy and in love with yourself and this life. There is meaning and a reason for this chapter of your life.

I felt compelled to write this because I want to help people. I want people to find the light and heal quicker than I did. I don't want people to suffer as long as I did. I hope, in any small way, the ideas in this book can be the spark that brings you back to life and help you say, "Thank God for depression."

Chapter One:

A NEW PERSPECTIVE
A Bush, Ayahuasca, and a Whole New World

I vomited in a bush somewhere on the grounds of a twelve-million-dollar ranch estate. I was wearing all white, looking more like a cult member than I was comfortable with, and high as hell on the psychedelic cactus San Pedro, a cousin of mescaline.

I jumped in the bush because a groundskeeper had just passed and I didn't want to raise suspicion. As he passed, I gave him my best, hey-look-at-me-I'm-just-a-friendly-so-ber-white-guy-wearing-all-white-not-about-to-vomit-in-your-bush wave. After he passed, I vomited and held my head, because life and nature around me were beginning to swirl, bend, and sway like a Salvador Dali painting on acid.

Nature was coming alive in the most magical and overwhelming way. Trees were winking at me. The grass was humming with such vivid consciousness it seemed like the blades were one note away from singing "heigh-ho" and carrying me away. I was holding on to the bush to ground and steady myself until I noticed that it, too, started to vibrate and smile at me.

It was the morning after my first Ayahuasca ceremony. The head of my then-record label had invited me and seven of her closest friends to sit with the medicine for her birthday. When I said yes, I had no idea what to expect. All I knew was that I was at the end of my rope with depression.

I was twenty-eight and lost in the depths of what I now call my Dead Decade, a ten-year-plus long journey of being, let's not sugarcoat it, kicked in the teeth by depression and anxiety.

Up until that point, I had considered depression the worst thing to ever happen to me. It had taken everything from me. It had destroyed my promising professional career as the lead singer of a rock band. It had robbed me of all my joy and happiness in life. It took hostage my belief system, my thoughts, and my self-worth.

I eventually came to believe that I didn't deserve to be alive and that nothing good would ever come of my life again. I felt like I had no future and I'd broken my life beyond repair. I had come to believe my life on earth was a mistake and that I was a meaningless lump of nothingness, alone in the universe. Depression left me terrified of everything, but most of all myself.

In a few short years, I went from confidently playing to crowds of forty thousand people to going into isolation, living back at my parents' house, and feeling ashamed to tell anyone I was a musician.

The last three years of it had been especially brutal, ravaged with physical pain and constant brain fog. Unable to write or think clearly, I was near suicidal daily.

Around then, I had finally hit a point where I said, "Fuck it." I gave up. Depression won.

I never thought for a single second I would ever come out of it. I believed myself to be depression incarnate and my identity on this planet was depression. Hope and healing were about as far off on my radar as an iPhone to a caveman.

So when the head of my record label called me up and said, "Do you want to do Ayahuasca?" I said, "Fuck yes." I then tried to cancel four times because I was absolutely terrified.

I had never done psychedelics before. I felt like I was already on such thin and shaky ground. Introducing a substance that invokes any other plane seemed like suicide and a permanent trip to the mental asylum.

Ironically, starting with Ayahuasca and San Pedro as your first psychedelic experience is kind of like someone offering you a joint and you saying, "No, I don't do drugs," then five minutes later you're freebasing meth on a corner in downtown LA.

Again, I said yes because I was at the end of my rope. I explored many routes to find relief from depression, and although I did find a lot that helped and learned a ton while making healthy steps forward, I felt like I needed something big and dramatic to change my life forever. I quickly learned when you ask for big and dramatic from Universe and the most powerful psychedelic plant medicine, big and dramatic are exactly what you get.

That yes led me to that bush on a twelve-acre estate, down on hands and knees, crawling because the leaves were laughing at me.

While this "Whoa, I'm on drugs, Mom, and that squirrel just gave me a download!" business is funny, the stark reality was that I was being faced with a crisis I'd never known. A really big, reality-shattering existential crisis.

It turned out that everything I knew about everything was wrong. Everything I thought I knew about reality, myself, my place in the world, my identity, God, life, and my own depression were entirely wrong.

There I was, vomiting in a bush, picking up the pieces of my rational mind, hiding from a gardener, hoping to God a centaur wouldn't appear and drag me to Narnia, and dealing with a personal reckoning that was both the most profoundly enlightening and most shattering experience of my entire life.

In this pivotal crisis, I was reconciling with the fact that it was over. My depression was gone. In two nights,

Ayahuasca had not only shown me the root of my own depression (which no amount of talk therapy would have gotten to the bottom of) but had cured me. She, Ayahuasca, wiped out my depression as casually as someone telling me where the nearest bathroom was.

What the Medicine Said

Ayahuasca, in her boundless intelligence, showed me that the root of my depression was simply a matter of being lost. Lost? It turned out that all of my depression was just a side effect of the pain of being lost from the divine. My depression was the pain of ignorance. I had forgotten who I was and where I came from.

My depression stemmed from the pain and forgetfulness of being spiritually ignorant of the truth of my real nature and connection to the divine. I didn't know I was lost.

Somewhere along the path of my life, I had forgotten my connection to God, Source, Divinity, whatever you want to call it, and the fact that we humans are divinity incarnate. We are quite literally slices of God walking around on earth, as sacred as sacred can get.

Two nights with this medicine had broken the trance and spell of over twenty years of wrong and ignorant thinking and led me home. I walked out of that ceremony a different person than the one who walked in.

I walked into that ceremony a grumpy, reluctant, and bummed-out atheist. I left with overwhelming proof, experiencing and knowing that God, Divinity, Universal Consciousness, Source, is real and ever-present always.

I walked in believing my life was a mistake and left knowing that the alignment of God and the universe is perfect. Everything happens for a reason and has a purpose. Absolutely nothing is out of place. I am exactly where I am supposed to be and am always exactly where I need to be. There are no mistakes.

I walked in believing myself to be outside of life, separate and alone in the universe, but then I had a powerful knowing that I was eternally guided; that even in the darkest depths of my depression, I was never alone. God, Divinity, the Guru, was right there with me, guiding me through every breath and step, through past, present, and future. That connection is always there and always accessible. We humans forget that sometimes.

I walked in feeling meaningless, and the medicine said, "You are God incarnate. So is every other person on the planet. We are composed of the same source material that God, Divinity, and consciousness are composed of. Every living being is made up of that source material that created the stars, flowers, animals, planets, and consciousness itself, and it's blissfully powerful. You are made of really powerful stuff."

I remember stopping to think, because I am divinity incarnate, if I hate myself, I hate God. If I'm mean to myself, I am being mean to God. If I love myself, I love God. How

I treat myself is a reflection of how I treat God. How I view myself is a reflection of how I see this life. It's the most simple idea of life as unity, oneness, and the universe being a mirror for how you see yourself.

I walked in thinking I was a burnt-out loser of a lead singer from a has-been rock band. Then the medicine showed me that my true nature was boundless consciousness. Our true nature as human beings is infinite and boundless joy and limitless bliss and expansion. Ego identification on earth is only part of the story.

I walked in thinking my mind and thoughts were king, but Ayahuasca showed me that our limited human intelligence is like a single speck of sand to the endless and infinite ocean of divinity. Peace is about being rather than thinking. The magnitude of God and consciousness is mega.

That's all I was thinking about puking in that bush, in full revelatory crisis mode. I was grappling and wrestling with big holy-shit ideas and the death of my old self. It was a complete overhaul of my entire belief system and perception of myself, reality, and the world. The medicine had given me a new worldview and a new sense of reality. I realized I'd spent the last decade attacking a symptom. Everything I ever knew was wrong, including my entire perception and relationship with depression.

My depression was no longer a thing of terror. It was a gift and my greatest teacher. It was a beacon, a warning, telling me something was wrong and missing in my life. It was a lighthouse and the necessary and prerequisite suffering for a spiritual homecoming and big healing to take place.

If depression led me to this bliss, this healing and change, how could it ever be a "bad" thing? Depression brought me back home to God, to life, to myself. It took a decade of hell, but the darkness cleared, and it was like I'd never seen the sun before. Thank God for depression.

The Most Important Question No One Asked You about Depression

If you read this story and thought, "Fantastic, I don't need this book, I'll just go slurp some Ayahuasca and all my depression will be gone." Hold on there, cowboy. First, I've known plenty of depressed people who have drank plant medicine and it hasn't helped.

Plant medicine is an answer, but not the answer for everyone. I am a huge plant medicine advocate for myself, but I cannot recommend it to anyone. Your path to healing is not my path to healing. Medicine has been integral and at the center of my own healing, but I also paired it with the other techniques you're going to read about in this book. It is magical, profound, and incredible in how it can facilitate deep inner work in ways that other modalities might not be able. However, you don't necessarily need it to get the same insights I got. Meditation retreats, therapy, and spiritual study can get you there. There are many different paths to the top of the mountain of healing, and plant medicine is just one of the possible paths. I'll get into all this later.

Second, it misses the entire point of my story, which is that everything I knew about my depression was wrong. In my blistering awakening, the relationship I had with depression was forever changed in an instant. Depression wasn't a terrorist. It was my greatest teacher and gift.

My point in starting with this story is for you to question and change the relationship you have with depression. I want you to change the way you think about your own depression and to offer you a new perspective. I want you to be open to the possibility that if I can find hope and healing, so can you.

What if everything you think or know about your own depression is entirely wrong? What if your depression isn't a bad or evil thing? What if your depression has intelligence and consciousness? What if your depression is trying to teach you something or show you something? What if it's trying to lead you somewhere? What if there is a big beautiful reason and meaning for your depression that you have no idea about yet? What if your depression is the best thing to ever happen to you? What if one day you will say, "Thank God for depression"?

Or let's get wild and crazy: What if depression is a means to an end, and there is an infinitely intelligent being out there using it as grist for the mill to make you the best version of yourself you can be? Or even wilder, what if your soul made a contract before you were even born that depression is a mandatory lesson for you to figure out in your life this time around?

Here's a wild question I bet no therapist, doctor, or friend has ever asked you: What is the relationship you have with your depression? It's a bizarre yet vital question because how we perceive our own depression directly affects the journey we take with it.

Imagine your depression is a being. How do you see it? Is it a dictator? A terrifying evil spirit? Is it the worst thing to ever happen to you, or a teacher or a gift? Is it a cause of terror and resistance? Is it an opportunity? Do you listen to it? Are you ashamed of it? Do you run from it?

What is depression trying to tell you at this very moment?

Perception Is Everything

The biggest freedom we have in life is the ability to consciously choose how to make meaning out of and perceive the world and everything that happens to us. We have this gift at every moment of our lives. Our perceptions essentially determine our entire lives and the paths we take.

Two people can get fired from their jobs; one loses their mind and drinks themselves into oblivion, and the other sees it as an opportunity for growth and to step into their full heart's purpose. Just like this, we get to consciously choose how we perceive our journey with depression.

Changing your mindset about depression changes your relationship with it and the path you take with it. If you choose to see depression as a terrorist and the worst thing to happen to you, odds are, you will feel like a victim, helpless, or you will fight and resist it and first-rate suffer. Panic stacks on panic and creates even more suffering. You will be terrified of it all the time and won't be still enough to actually receive the help you need.

If you choose to see depression as a teacher and a gift, you can cocreate a life with depression, trust that it is here for a reason and ask it, "What do you have to teach me today, and where will you guide me?" When you wake up and feel depressed, you can say, "Oh, what a beautiful opportunity to learn how to listen to my body and spirit, love myself, and take better care of myself today." It alchemizes panic, dread, and shame into better self-care. Fighting and resisting lead to different results than trust and faith. When you make this shift, you change your energy from resistance to acceptance, and the world responds to that almost immediately. It's radical.

Maybe you don't really know anything about your own depression, why it's here, where it came from, how long it will last, or what it's here to teach you, and that's a-ok. I just want to open your mind to start perceiving your own mental health journey in a new light, one that is working with you instead of against you.

Depression Is a Teacher

What would happen right now if you chose to see your depression as a wise teacher? If you stopped reading and asked, "Depression, what are you trying to teach me today? What are you trying to teach me in this very moment?"

If you choose to see depression as a teacher, you can start to tune into its intelligence and consciousness. You can listen to it and get curious. Your depression is here for a reason. Maybe it's here to help you grow, guide you home, or make you into the person you were always meant to be.

Maybe it's trying to tell you something is wrong or show you something about your life that needs to change. Maybe something is lacking or missing?

Maybe depression is trying to lead you somewhere. To where and to what? That's for you to find out. When you are open to this idea, the next question is, will you resist it, or will you listen and act?

The truth is you have no idea if depression in your life is a good or bad thing yet because you don't know where it's leading you.

Although it probably doesn't seem like it, depression is both growth and healing. When we learn how to get still and listen to our inner depths, which I'll teach you later, we can start to access the gifts depression has to offer us.

At their core, depression and anxiety are intimate opportunities to learn more about ourselves, who we are, what our work is, and what we really need. We then learn how to take better take care of ourselves. This is exciting because we get to find out what's there and how we can change it.

Although it took me a decade of suffering and a boatload of psychedelics to get to this point, I now count depression and anxiety as some of my most powerful teachers in life. They have taught me about life and reminded me of how sacred and strong I am. They have tested me and led me on a spiritual path. They have shown me how much of a gift this life is and how sacred being in this existence is.

Depression Is a Gift

What would happen right now if you chose to see your depression as a gift? What if you could trust that one day you will wake up so in love with life and so in love with who you are that depression will be the best thing to ever happen to you? Trust that it's working with you, not against you. What if depression is just a stepping stone toward the big and beautiful person you are truly meant to be?

Suffering from depression led me on a spiritual path and was the catalyst for my spiritual awakening. Without that pain, I would never have had the urge to explore anything spiritual. My journey with yoga, meditation, Transcendental Meditation, spiritual texts, and plant medicine would never have happened without depression. I've had experiences so profound and blissfully meaningful that it made every single second of depression and anxiety worth it to get there. It also led me to sobriety, therapy, and new relationships, and now, especially, as I write this book, depression has evolved into another gift. I can help people heal in their own journey. In these ways, my depression is a gift and has a purpose, and I know yours is and does too.

Suffering can be a requisite for healing. Most times, we can't have healing without suffering. The pain forces us toward the light.

Some say, "Your biggest wound is your biggest gift." This is true for your depression as well.

Trust

I want to emphasize the importance of trust and faith. I repeat these ideas because they are powerful perspective shifts that take repetition to really land. Trust that there is a reason for your depression. Trust that depression is leading you somewhere. Trust that depression is a gift and a teacher. Trust that a power greater than you has brought depression into your life to teach you and show you something. Trust that your soul is on a journey of evolution, and depression is a pitstop on that path.

Trust that you are being guided right now, and trust that something way bigger than you and way smarter than you is making the plans for your life. Those plans are so blissful and wild that you could never have imagined them or thought of them for yourself. There is an intelligence (call it God, Spirit, Universal Intelligence) who is with you right now at this very moment, at every breath, walking this path with you and keeping you safe. Put your life and healing in the hands of something bigger. What do you have to lose?

A New Worldview

I want to end this chapter by sharing my worldview with you. It's helpful to be offered a new perspective because I know how hopeless and limiting depression and anxiety can be. Some of these parts I've echoed earlier, but I want to present them in their entirety as a mantra, so you can come back to it when you're feeling lost.

I also want you to remember that this is a worldview from me, someone who never thought he would overcome depression or, quite frankly, live past thirty. I struggled, suffered, and fell headfirst into every pitfall and mistake a person can make. I felt alone and meaningless for over ten years.

If I can come out of depression better, stronger, and wiser, I believe anyone can. Healing is possible. That is everyone's right. I somehow made that long journey home, and you can too.

I'm not claiming to be a spiritual teacher, but I think we sometimes get lulled into the illusion that people who write self-help books came out of the womb perfect, Instagram-able, enlightened beings who open their mouths and vomit out wisdom. It's hard to relate to that. We also forget that they too poop, occasionally yell at their printers, eat too many doughnuts, and might have weird porn caches— all to say they are ordinary people too, in no way different than you.

We create our own worlds. Whatever lens we choose to see the world through is going to affect what we see. Depression has a certain lens, and it's different from a lens of faith and divinity. What Ayahuasca gave me was a new lens through which to see the world, and I am here to share that with you.

My Mantra

I believe in a perfect, all-loving, infinite, and eternal divine intelligence in the universe that created us. This spiritual and energetic force (call it whatever you want, Divinity, God, Source, Unity, the Guru, Divine Mother) is guiding us every breath and step of our lives. Into the seemingly mundane and mystical. Whether our search is for parking spots or overall life purpose, this force is always walking with us.

This Divinity, this Source, is composed of everything. You are composed of the same matter that built the stars, the universe, plants, chia pets, you name it. You are a part of everything, connected to everything. Life is in you and could not exist without you.

There is a sense of oneness to this. We all come from this Source, this Unity, this pure consciousness whose intrinsic nature is love, joy, and bliss. This Source is infinite, boundless, limitless, and powerful. It's a place of being, beyond the mind. We come from a place of boundless joy, and our true nature is eternal bliss. And you, personally, emanate from that. You are created from that. Your true nature is love, joy, and bliss.

In this sense, I believe your truest identity is spirit; you are an infinite and eternal soul. You are divinity incarnate, an eternal spirit having a human experience. Your identity is both Beth, who works in shoe sales, and Spirit, an incarnate piece of God.

I believe the alignment of the universe is perfect. I believe there are no mistakes, no accidents, and that everything is for a reason. I believe at every step, every breath along the way, we are always guided by Divinity. Even in our darkest moments, Divinity is here with us, always accessible.

I believe with all my heart that there is a purpose for why you are here. There is a reason you were born into this incarnation, this physical body, the family you were born into, those problems you have. Your soul, your spirit, chose this exact time and place to be alive on planet Earth, the school of Earth, for the lessons you needed to learn.

Depression is both a lesson and a teacher. You were meant to be here. It's no accident. Maybe you don't know what the reason is yet. But I know there is a reason for it, and one day, you will see it with love and compassion.

I believe there is a plan for your life, so perfect and guided that when healing does come, you'll know it was at the exact time and place you needed and that you were ready. You'll look at all the past moments of darkness and realize they were necessary steps for this blissful moment of healing to come. You'll realize that everything you did and didn't do led you up to that moment, and you will be overwhelmingly thankful for all of it.

I write this not from intellect or rationality but with knowing certainty, from all of my cells, from my being. There is too much light inside of you not to make its way to the surface. Your true nature is love, light, and boundless and limitless bliss and joy.

Consider that a perfect and loving divine force is writing your story and has a path and purpose for your life so beautiful and big that you could never have foreseen it or planned it alone. This plan is in motion now.

There is an end date to the pain. It's temporary. Depression is only a chapter in your life, not the entire novel. More importantly, it's not who you are, not who you ever were, and won't be who you will be.

There is a reason and purpose for your suffering. You will not only overcome this depression, but one day you will wake up and be overwhelmingly thankful for all of it because of who it has made you. In this moment, no matter what it entails, you are right where you're supposed to be.

One day I know you'll wake up and love your life so much that you wouldn't take back anything that led you here, and you'll say, "Thank God for depression."

Now let's roll up our sleeves and punch depression in the face.

Ways to Integrate This Chapter

- Read the mantra daily.
- *Journal Prompt:* Free write on the question, "What is the relationship I have with depression?" Imagine depression is a being, and you're having a conversation with it. If you're having trouble answering this, write a letter to depression, detailing all your feelings and emotions about it. Be honest, and don't hold back.
- If you're having a hard day, put down your phone, take three deep breaths, and ask, "Depression, what are you trying to teach me right now? What are you trying to tell me? Where is the lesson here?"
- *Journal Prompt:* Write out five ways your depression could be a gift. How has it made you a better person? How has it led you to good things?
- *Journal Prompt:* Write out five ways your depression is a teacher. What has it taught you so far?

Chapter Two:
FIRST STEPS
The Do's of Depression

I can't think of a bigger letdown in my life than getting off a tour with my rock band.

Rock band, you say? Well, yes. Against the rational advice of everyone in my life, I started a rock band called Beware of Darkness when I was eighteen. It began with just a drummer and me, three hundred dollars cash, and a garage turned home recording studio the owner hand-dug out on a meth binge. Within a year, we were signed, made our first record, and began touring. This was the beginning of a ten-year adventure in rock star life: touring the world with some of my favorite bands, making records, producing a top-five rock radio hit, and "living both the dream and the nightmare" in a ton of ways. The tours were the best part, but also the hardest.

The entire tour, you feel like a demigod on stage, an unfuckwithable and invincible pirate traveling the world. You're a big deal. You're playing original songs in front of hundreds of fans who adore you. Fans buy tickets and merch, then hand you drinks and give you the "secret" handshake as they slide God-knows-what kind of plastic baggie'd drug into your hand. Everyone wants a picture with you. They ask you to sign boobs or thighs and might even get your signature or band logo tattooed on them.

Touring gives you a huge sense of purpose. You feel like you matter and you're doing something exciting with your life. You have places to be and a tight schedule to stick to. You're living a rambunctious life on a fast-moving train, leaving cities behind with the abandon of a billionaire dropping a dollar.

Then, like all things, the tour ends. The next thing you know, the tour manager drops you off with all your gear, and you find yourself back at your parents' house, alone, folding your underwear, wondering why the hell no one is clapping for you. All the confidence, bravado, swagger, excitement, and fun are gone from your life almost immediately. As you're standing in line waiting at the supermarket to buy food for your empty fridge, it seems like another lifetime that a week ago people were cheering for you and handing you LSD in the club bathroom.

It can be a devastating shock. After years of touring

experience, I came to fully understand the nature of post-tour depression.

A year before that miracle Ayahuasca healing I told you about, I had just finished a tour and found myself face to face with impending post-tour depression.

As I got dropped off back home in Santa Barbara, I vowed this time would be different. I wouldn't let post-tour depression win. I had a genius plan: I'd keep the party going. If I never stopped moving, kept going out and drinking, I would never be still enough to feel the sadness and letdown of post-tour depression, right?

My brilliant idea for dealing with post-tour depression was also the one and only method I had used against depression my entire life: avoidance. If I don't admit I have a problem, avoid it, and hide, hopefully things will magically get better, I believed. I'd then hope to God the next depressive episode wouldn't be as bad as the last. In other words, when I finished this specific tour, I dealt with it by getting wasted.

One Tuesday night, I found myself very, very drunk in a bar in Santa Barbara called the Wildcat Lounge, whose ambiance could make a construction site porta-potty seem like a Michelin-rated restaurant.

The bar was so packed you could barely move. Hip hop was vibrating my rib cage. Most men around me had the nervous and desperate energy of trying to find something or someone to stick their dick into. Most girls were looking around wondering why the hell they were there. And as I pissed in a urinal that wouldn't stop moving, the only thoughts in my head were, I want to die, I want to kill myself, I'm done with life. I wasn't exactly putting out the Hey-ladies,-I'm-a-guy-you-want-to-sleep-with energy.

After I drove home drunk that night again, which was becoming a regular routine, I got in bed, smoked weed to oblivion, and prayed. Drunk prayed. Except it felt more like I was making demands. I was begging God to kill me. I was begging him to take my life. I was writhing in bed, and with every cell of my being, I kept repeating over and over again, "I don't want this life. Kill me. I'm done with this. I don't want to be here. Life is not for me."

When I woke up the next day, I went to a coffee shop and cried under my big cool dark rock star sunglasses. I called my mom and told her what had happened. She told me to stop drinking. I did.

I hit my bottom. Ten years of running from depression led me to that point.

Drinking was my last frontier in avoiding my depression. I did everything to fix my depression without actually facing it. I now had nothing left to hide behind. I felt exposed and confused. I was finally too exhausted and broken to fight anymore. It shocked me what came next.

Within a few weeks, I found myself in a doctor's office, finally open to antidepressants, and a therapist synchronistically came into my life. They both saved my life.

As soon as I stopped running and faced my pain, the universe responded alarmingly quick. When I let go of the stories and finally knelt to admit, "I need help; I am suffering; I am in pain and don't know what to do," life brought people in to help me at lightning speed. It was kind of like the universe was just waiting for me behind the curtains the entire time, and as soon as I gave the go-ahead, she immediately did her thing.

The Do's of Depression

I know that not everyone reading this is a rock star with post-tour depression, but I can guess you might be making the same mistakes I made in trying to cope with depression. I don't want you to be like me. I don't want you to take as much time to find healing as I did.

This chapter is about the first steps you can take with depression. I'm going to offer some simple do's and a few more perspective shifts that will hopefully make your journey with depression a bit easier and less lengthy. I want you to find the light quicker than I did. How great would it be if my ten years was your six months?

Do: Please Be Kind To Yourself

When I was depressed, people asked me if I was dating anyone, and the answer was always, "No, I'm too busy being in an abusive relationship with myself to have time for anyone else."

The path out of depression is not self-brutality and macho aggression. The path out of depression is gentleness, self-compassion, and love.

We can't heal from depression with the same energy that keeps us stuck in it. Fear, lack, scarcity, anger, and shame will keep us lost in loops of self-abuse and self-abandonment. Love, trust, faith, dedication, surrender, and openness are ultimately what will save us.

Self-compassion is the name of the game as you read this book and take your depression journey (and in your life in general). Learning how to champion ourselves, be our own biggest fan and supporter, and be the gentle guardian and protector of our heart, spirit, and soul makes all the difference in our mental health path.

The first time my therapist mentioned the idea of self-compassion, I balked. "Me? Love myself? There's absolutely nothing good about me to love."

Depression can make self-compassion difficult for a lot of reasons we will go into later. Self-compassion can be an alien concept when we are used to berating ourselves, but it's absolutely necessary for us to find healing.

Yes, this book is about depression, but on a deeper level, it's about the relationship we have with ourselves.

Depression can make us enemies of ourselves, hate ourselves, and wish we were different. Being mean or brutal with ourselves is a guarantee we will suffer more.

So please, please, please, be kind to yourself. Practice learning how to love yourself, be kind to yourself, and champion yourself.

We often don't treat others the way we treat ourselves. If a friend comes to us for help, saying, "I'm sad," we most likely offer them support, presence, and love. We wouldn't blame them for being weak or add judgment, making them feel worse than they did before coming to us. Yet often, this is exactly how we treat ourselves with depression. We punish and torture ourselves for feeling like we do, adding resistance and unnecessary suffering. Now reflect this back to yourself. You are that hurting person. How do you treat yourself when you are going through it?

Treat yourself like you'd treat a sick child or a puppy. They need love, support, and tenderness. So do you. You wouldn't berate them or punish them for their moods, thoughts, and behaviors.

Gentleness is the way to hold yourself as you read this book. As you begin to implement the ideas, love and acceptance are what you need, not shame and judgment.

Our lives will start to change in big ways when we begin to regard ourselves as someone worthy of life, happiness, and grace, someone worth saving, and someone lovable and capable of making mistakes.

Don't use this book as another excuse for you to punish yourself. Use this book as a friend and a guide. If you are punishing yourself for having depression, please stop. If you are punishing yourself for anything in your life, please stop.

Integrate: "I Love This Part Too" Meditation Practice

If you are having a hard time being kind to yourself, this meditation is a great way to practice self-compassion.

We all have a shadow and things about ourselves and our lives we don't like or aren't proud of. Depression and negative thinking can terrorize us and punish us for these traits and send us spiraling. We hate how we look, where we are stuck in our lives, our situations, our moods, and so on.

Whenever we don't feel enough, or feel unworthy or sad, or are being mean to ourselves, we can pause, put our hands on our heart, and say, "I love this part of me too."

Embracing whatever comes up and dousing it in love can offer us immediate relief and is an easy act of self-compassion we can practice anywhere, anytime. Love and self-compassion have the power to dissolve shadow, darkness, and depression. Chastisement and inner judgment don't produce the same fruit as self-compassion and love. When we start to love the darkest parts of ourselves, we begin to bring about positive change in our lives.

Do: Focus on the Path, Not the Outcome

I never in a million years would have guessed that drinking the tea of an Amazonian vine, traveling across the universe, and having visions of breastfeeding plant saplings would bring me out of depression. I also never could have guessed that the wild and wacky path of being a lead singer in a rock band would lead me there.

The good news is you also don't know how long your depression will last or what will pull you out of it. It's none of your business. Thank God. This is reason to celebrate.

Throughout my twenties, I spent so much time hating that I was depressed and worrying about when my depression would end that it frazzled me to the point of inability to act. This only made everything worse.

When we focus on the outcome, we suffer. We never know how things will work out. We just have to show up and see what happens.

When we are suffering and depressed, our ego just wants the pain to stop and wants control over the outcome. We want to know what will end our pain and panic when we don't know. When we don't feel in control over our own suffering, we feel powerless and scared.

This panic creates resistance, takes us out of the present moment, and creates secondary fires like anger, fear, confusion, and sadness. This paradoxically keeps us from making any meaningful changes that will actually spring us out of depression because we are dealing with our resistance instead of the actual core problem at hand.

Fretting and worrying about what will pull us out of depression takes us out of the present moment, which is the one place we can actually do something about our depression.

Life is all about the path, and the path is always the present moment. When we focus on this, we flow. When we let go of the need to know how and when our depression will end, we let go of the fight, the resistance, and the struggle to control the end of the story. We can then can start to be present for the path and journey and work with what's here and now. All change is born in the present moment, and when we accept what is here right now, we can begin to rewrite the story of our lives.

Letting go of our need to control the outcome is a practice in trust and the first step in inviting healthy and positive change. Letting go of the outcome means you trust you are being guided, and you are walking together on a journey with depression and divinity.

Focusing on the outcome takes us out of our hearts and into our heads. Focusing on the path brings us back into our hearts, bodies, and souls. My friend Troy Byer said one of my favorite lines of all time, "When I come from ego, nothing works. When I come from spirit, everything works." Ego wants to know the outcome; spirit enjoys and trusts the path.

I guarantee that your mind cannot think of a better outcome than the one the universe has planned for you. Your brain is depressed and probably already overwhelmed and fried right now, so don't give it the extra pressure of figuring out what will fix you and when. Offer it up to a higher power. Give it to God.

What if not knowing how your life will turn out isn't a source of anxiety but of awe, wonder, and excitement because it means that life has planned some outcome and path so beautiful and blissful, you never could have planned it alone?

The truth is that at any moment in your life, infinite possibilities exist for what could happen to you next. Tomorrow, someone or something could come into your life and change everything. We never know what will happen.

I've never written a book before, and the process has been the toughest of my life. This past month I've been frustrated because I just want to be finished writing it. I had no idea how long it would take. I started to panic about it and set unrealistic deadlines. Ironically, I got so stressed and frazzled about the outcome, it left me unable to write a single word.

I was stuck in this mud for weeks until a friend of mine reminded me that writing is a form of meditation. I realized at that point how stuck I'd been and how focusing on the outcome had not only sent me into a total panic but had also destroyed the beauty and joy of the actual process.

I got centered and reminded myself that every time I sit down to write is a prayer. It's my job to get out of the way and just show up because everyday I have no idea what will come out on the page. I had to remind myself it's a meditation and a form of channeling. When I got into this space, the ideas, words, and inspiration flew through me. Then I didn't panic at all because I was in the present moment, being with whatever was on the page in front of me. The book and its process were teaching me, and it would be done when it was done, just like your depression.

When we wake up and feel depressed, we have two options. We can say, "Depressed again, I hate this. I hate myself. When will this end? I want this to be done." This creates resistance, self-loathing, and suffering.

Or we wake up and say, "Depressed again, okay. I will make today a prayer. Depression, teach and show me whatever I need to know today. My intention is to be as present and gentle with myself as possible. Let me see where this takes me today. Let me get curious. Maybe there's an avenue I'm not exploring yet. Maybe someone will come into my life and bring the help I need."

Life is a form of meditation. Everything we do can be a prayer. Wisdom, opportunity, healing, life, and divinity are being channeled through you at all times. We just have to tune into the present moment to receive it. Offer up your outcome to a power greater than yourself.

Integrate:

> Take your journey with depression one day, or even one moment, at a time. If you feel overwhelmed, ask yourself, "What is the next right action here? What can I do right now or today that will help me?"

Do: Try Everything You Can—An All-Hands-On-Deck Approach

You don't know what the magic bullet is for you to emerge from your depression, and you don't have to know. Your job is to walk the path and show up for opportunities. You must have a combination of faith and action. I recommend an all-hands-on-deck approach for moving through depression. That means taking full responsibility for your life and actions. It means being open to and doing everything you can while knowing and trusting in your heart that a power and intelligence bigger than you is guiding you.

What pulls you out of it could be a combination of things we will talk about. It could be a single night with Ayahuasca or two years of taking medicine. It could be yoga, therapy, antidepressants, leaving a job, changing your diet, breaking up with that shitty boyfriend, or moving. It could be changing how you see your identity and how you see your place in the universe, spiritual study, or a combination of all of these things. What pulls you out of it could be as quick as getting hit by lighting or as slow as a continuous drip of water wearing away a rock over the years. This entire process could last six months or six years.

Because you don't know what will pull you out of it, be open to anything. Try it all. There is always an unexplored avenue. "Nothing works" is never an excuse. There's always something new we can do.

If you feel like you're getting stuck again or nothing is working, don't stop or give up. Try other things, pivot, and look honestly at your own stories and actions. If what you try doesn't work, don't get lost in a story about how nothing is working. Just keep opening your eyes wider for something else that might help. You just haven't found what will heal you yet.

Faith and action. Tackling depression is a combination of these two. You are going to do everything you possibly can and explore every avenue that might offer the possibility of help while offering your path up to God. Do the daily footwork and remember that you are always right where you are meant to be.

Think of your depression as an exploration and journey. Depression is taking you somewhere. It's your job to walk the journey with depression moment by moment.

When we start to be open to different paths and mindsets, take action, and make a commitment to open our minds and our hearts to change and healing, the universe hears it and responds. Often just trying something new or doing something differently is enough to change the way the universe responds to you. You're changing your energy, and life responds to this.

The daily inner and outer work you do rearranges energy and clears the stage for divinity and the universe to do its magic. And be ready, because when you begin to clear out the cobwebs, the universe will move quicker than you think.

Integrate:

- Write down ten different paths you could explore that might offer relief from depression (meditation courses, books, yoga, etc.). If you can't think of any, Google it, or ask a friend you trust.

- Pray daily for guidance, wisdom, and courage.

- Write down ten small actions you can take that will help you on your mental health journey. They can be as small as making your bed or making sure you eat enough.

Everything matters

Here's the most important thing to remember for the all-hands-on-deck approach: Everything matters. Everything affects everything, no matter the size. Your action today leads to you where you are meant to be tomorrow. There is no such thing as insignificant or a waste of time. Things we think are small can have the biggest impact, and things we think will be slam dunks might be airballs. We don't know what works until we try it and are in the present moment with it. We might as well just be open and show up and see.

When I toured with my band, sometimes the worst sound checks led to the best shows, and the best sound checks led to shows that were an absolute disaster. I realized there was no way to predict how a show would go based on how well things were going before. I learned I just had to show up, be open, and see what happened, taking everything as it came.

Everything you do in terms of healing is a stepping stone for something else to take place. Remember you are being guided, so trust that everything you do now, even if you consider it a mistake or failure, is a lesson that is leading you where you are meant to be.

Actions such as getting sober, doing yoga, eating healthier, and honoring your sleep may not magically thrust you out of depression overnight. Trust that they are slow builds that shift your mindset and energetically put your body, spirit, and heart back in alignment to set the stage and clear the path for the universe to swoop in and initiate bigger healing. There's a lot of power in the "tiny" things.

When I had that mind-blowing experience with Ayahuasca that brought me out of depression, I looked back on every experience before it and saw them as necessary for my awakening.

So besides potentially plant medicine, I don't think there's a single instant cure-all for depression or anxiety. Rather, it's making a commitment to a combination of a lot of small daily practices and unsexy activities, cultivating new mindsets, and creating habits that will heal and help you. And when you dive into things like this—changing behaviors, habits, beliefs, and consciousness—it's a marathon, not a sprint.

Do: Shed The Stories around Depression

Depression is never just depression. At least for me it wasn't. Depression was also the handful of brutal narratives around what I thought it meant for me as a person to be depressed.

I thought being depressed meant there was something fundamentally wrong with me. I thought it meant that I was broken beyond repair. I thought it meant I was weak, less than, lazy, and meaningless. I thought it made me stained, unworthy of anything good happening in my life.

I was also hit hard as hell with stories about what it meant to be a depressed male. I had this toxic idea that, as a male, showing emotion or vulnerability was a weakness. I thought I had to keep it together at all times. I had to always be "on." I wasn't allowed to be hurt or appear weak. I also felt ashamed that I wasn't strong enough to fix myself on my own.

Because of these beliefs, admitting or telling anyone else I was depressed felt like the biggest failure of my life.

This is why I ran. Admitting I was depressed out loud meant all my worst fears about myself were true. I had so much shame around these stories it took me ten years to admit I was depressed to anyone. My own inner judgment, paired with the fear of people's potential judgment, led me to silence.

What are your stories around depression? What does it mean to you to be depressed? What do you think depression means about you? If you have stories around depression and what that means, examine that. We must reframe the stories we tell ourselves about depression.

Being depressed doesn't mean you are broken. It doesn't mean you are lacking in any way. Being depressed doesn't mean you are weak (in fact, I think it means you're incredibly strong). Being depressed doesn't take away any of the brilliant splendor of your magnificence of being a human on this planet. Being depressed doesn't tarnish your soul, and it's not your identity. There is nothing wrong with you because you are depressed.

Remember, we get to consciously choose our own perspective in life. Being depressed can mean whatever you want it to mean. Being depressed doesn't really mean anything other than the meaning and value you give it. We have the power to create and shed our own stories about depression.

Healing, the spiritual path, and the road to happiness are all about shedding. Shed any of the stories about depression that don't serve you. Shed the shame, shed the outcome, shed the unhealthy ways of coping, and shed the avoidance. Come back to trust and self-compassion.

It's hell enough being depressed, and we don't need to compound that with brutal stories about what we think it means to be depressed.

Integrate:

Write out the stories you are telling about your depression and what it means to you and about you. Next, take these questions and examine them. For every story you have, ask the question:

- What is the underlying belief here?
- Is this true? A fact?
- What is a positive and kind rewrite for this story?
- If the story is, "Depression means I'm broken," the positive affirmation and kind reframe is "I am whole."

Do: Notice

Notice the thoughts and emotions that come up for you as you read this book. This book is a mirror. It will show you where you are stuck or blocked. It will reveal your belief system to you. If you're reading this book, start to notice thoughts or excuses like:

- "I can't <insert excuse here> because of < other lame excuse. >"
- The famous, "Yeah but," <insert excuse why it would work for anyone else but you. >"
- "This guy's an idiot, fuck this guy and all his bullshit."
- "Oh, he's bringing God into this? I'm out."

Whenever you catch yourself in one of these patterns, celebrate. You just found a limiting belief or unhelpful thought. A big part of this book is about becoming aware of our own self-limiting thoughts and beliefs so we can consciously begin to rewrite them.

Integrate:

Write down your thoughts, negative or positive, as they come up as you read. Later in the book, I will teach you how to rewrite thoughts, but for now I just want you to notice.

Do: Stop Running

The hands-down dumbest mistake I ever made with my depression was running from it. It cost me my twenties and kept me from getting any help.

All running and avoiding do is create more suffering by creating more problems than solutions. Our pain only gets worse. It's also exhausting. Don't run from your depression.

Why we run

When we want to run, the biggest questions to ask are, what are we unwilling to feel, and what are we actually running from? What's the fear or emotion behind the desire to avoid or run? What do we have to gain by running? What do we have to gain by being still and facing our pain? What does facing our pain even mean? What do we think will happen?

I ran because I was terrified. I was terrified to admit to myself I was in pain or that I had a problem with depression. I wasn't ready to be with my own suffering or be alone with myself. Because of that, I tried to fix my pain in every way I could think of without actually facing myself or the pain. If I never had to admit to myself something was wrong, I didn't have a problem. It's the same sort of tactic as the "you can't get a STD if you don't get tested." Not actually true.

Why running doesn't work

The biggest downfall of running is that you don't heal. Avoiding and running do not give us the stillness, acceptance, and presence necessary for us to find healing. The sooner you stop running, the quicker you will find healing.

When you run, you tend to cope in ways that don't help. There are two ways of coping with suffering: ways that help and ways that don't.

What's easy in the short term might hurt you in the long run. What's hard in the short term might help you in the long run.

Ways that don't help tend to be quick fixes that bring instant relief in the short term but hurt you in the long term. Drinking, video games, getting high, and so forth. These methods don't really fix your problems; they just pacify the symptoms of the problem and ironically bring about more pain and suffering.

I thought, maybe if my rock band gets famous I'll feel better. Maybe if I make money. Maybe if I get more followers. Maybe if I do a yoga teacher training, or if I get high or drunk enough, or date the right person, it'll fill the void and pain, and the burden of being alive will disappear. Of course, it goes without saying that none of this worked.

The irony is that trying to cope in unhealthy ways only compounded my suffering and created more pain. Now I was semi-famous, with a good chunk of money, and still depressed, which created more problems and new trauma that I still saw through the lens of depression.

A really bonkers thing that humans do is try to fix and heal the pain in ways that don't really fix the pain. Our fear of the actual pain is so much worse than the pain itself. We are so afraid of being with ourselves in our tenderness that we go to extreme lengths to avoid it, which ironically creates so much more suffering than the initial pain we were trying to run from.

It takes a lot of courage to be willing to face our own pain. It's terrifying, and we think we are going to die if we actually come face to face with our pain, but we won't.

It's safe to feel our own suffering, and it's freedom. Facing your pain, your emotions, and your feelings is always the way out. Don't run; feel the pain. You won't die.

Then there are coping mechanisms that work. These are things that are uncomfortable in the short term but help you in the long run. These are therapy, exercise, plant medicine, and the like. Healthy coping mechanisms get to the root, cause you to face your pain, and bring actual healing and change.

Without judgment, take a look at your current coping methods. What are they? Are they really addressing your depression? Are they working? Are they bringing about positive change? If not, maybe it's time to explore some other options.

We do the best we can with whatever coping mechanisms we have at the time, and when we find a better and healthier way, we can step into it. Don't beat yourself up if your coping mechanisms aren't the best. What is the solution to running? Full-blown acceptance.

Antidote for running: admit, allow, and accept

The sooner we admit and accept our pain, the sooner we allow healing to come in. When we resist and fight our depression, it prolongs our suffering. Admit, allow, and accept your depression.

Give your depression space to be here. Allow it to come

with its message, teachings, and wisdom. You don't have to "like" or "love" where you are, but full-blown acceptance—whatever is here in this moment, your truth—is the way to move through difficult situations.

Accepting your depression means you honor it, respect it, and see it. Acceptance means you are choosing courage and freedom, not fear. In AA, accepting and admitting is the first step, and it's the same with depression.

Often, getting on our knees with full acceptance and a humble willingness to ask the universe for help is the exact moment when the universe begins to help us.

Let's pray and ask for the courage to face our pain head-on. To confront ourselves with love and compassion. It's brave to ask for help. It takes courage to admit to someone you are suffering and in pain.

You're allowed to be depressed. It's ok, and it's safe to be depressed. You're allowed to feel this terrible weight. It's ok to not be ok. You're allowed to sit with it and be in it. You're allowed to be a wreck. You are safe as you are. You are perfect as you are at your core. Allow yourself the space to feel your suffering and pain. Feel all of it without story or judgment; the grief, the sadness, and the brokenness. Just be with it.

Accept yourself fully, however you are showing up in this moment. Even if you feel broken or sad, you are perfect.

Don't fake it. Don't resist. Let go of the armor, the defenses, the lies. You don't need to have anything together or put on a show.

Give the people in your life a gift by showing up exactly as you are. Even in what you think is your worst state, you are still a blessing to someone else.

Integrate:

In what ways are you running from depression? What emotion, fear, or belief is behind that?

Write out three healthy ways you are coping with depression and three unhealthy ways you are coping with depression.

Do: Prioritize Your Mental Health

A few years back, I was doing a podcast with probably the most genuine person of all time. He was about as sincere as they come, loved music above everything else, and was holding space for the interview with some of the most heartfelt and thoughtful questions I've ever been asked. I, meanwhile, felt about as lovable as a vat of acid because of my depression. One question he asked wrecked me.

He asked, "You did all this amazing stuff in such a short amount of time. You played for Conan, toured with the Smashing Pumpkins and Alice in Chains, played with Soundgarden, toured the world, and had a top-five rock hit. Do you wake up every morning and think, I did it? I made it. I'm successful."

The question shook me to the core in a heartbreaking way.

Despite experiencing that once-in-a-lifetime success that most people and garage bands only dream of, I still felt like a total failure. I had never once for a moment thought of myself as successful or "making it."

Depression had left me feeling so deeply unworthy of life, of existence, that the idea of celebrating any of my success felt ridiculous. I thought I didn't deserve to be alive, so how could I feel worthy of anything good happening in my life? I got the fame, the money, and still felt less-than. I felt devastated and empty despite everything I'd achieved. I paused and thought, How the hell am I going to answer this?

Dealing with mental health is like owing a debt to the mafia—if you don't take care of your mental health now, it will take care of you later. Sound mental health is the foundation for everything else in this life.

What are success, family, money, and fame worth if we don't have our mental health in place first to be present for them? They are all meaningless if we don't have our mental health. It's hard to enjoy anything when you're in the pit of depression. Focus all your energy on getting out of the pit, and then you can start to enjoy this life again.

Make your mental health your number one priority. Treat it like a full-time job. Everything in your life revolves around what serves your mental health. If something is hurting your mental health, let it go. There will be a time when you can relax, but for right now, make clearing up mental health your life purpose.

We can always get our careers back, but what about our mental health? Our well-being and mental health are too precious to squander, considering how little time we have here on the planet. Take the time to heal now before you are forced to later.

Integrate:

> What are three small actions you can take this week to prioritize healing on your mental health journey? Examples: making an appointment to see a therapist or reading this book!
>
> In what ways are you avoiding prioritizing your mental health?

Do: Be Willing to Fall Apart

Be willing to fall apart. By this I mean be willing to let go of whatever doesn't serve you in order to find the light.

Healing from depression is both a death and rebirth. It's the death of your old self and your old ways of doing things. It's the birth of an entirely new way of being. We need to be willing to die in order to find the light. This can feel like your life is falling apart.

If we want to have a different life, we need to do different things. Old patterns and old ways of being bring about the same old results. When we stay stuck in the known, nothing new ever happens in our lives. We sometimes trust and cling to the known because it feels "safer." In reality, it does more damage than good because it keeps us from healing. In this case, depression is the known, and what we need the most is the unknown.

Make love with the unknown

Having your life fall apart is not something to fear; it's a beautiful and exciting opportunity for rebirth. If we fear it, it's because we don't trust the unknown. We don't trust it because we have no control over what will happen to us if we step into the unknown. If that's the case, then it's our relationship with the unknown that needs work.

Our relationship with the unknown determines the quality of our lives. We need to learn how to trust the unknown because healing and the life of our dreams are found within it.

If we want change, we might need to let go of things that seem scary to live without: familiar jobs, living spaces, practices, addictions, routines, partnerships, vocations, etc. This might feel like death.

Ask yourself right now: How is your life serving you? How is your known working out for you? Would you be happy if things continued along in the same direction, or do you want big change and newness?

What are you even holding onto right now anyway? Are you happy with the life you are "keeping together" right now? What do you have to gain by staying stuck in old ways and patterns?

Sometimes we can be so focused on keeping it all together, going along with external expectations, or playing the game society wants us to play that we rarely give ourselves space or permission to fall apart. If we aren't really happy or fulfilled, what are we actually afraid of when it comes to falling apart? Is the cost of letting your life fall apart more than living in the chronic pain you're in?

Would it be worth it to take a big step back and explore healing rather than keep a broken train running?

Integrate:

Write about anything in your life you are holding onto that might be hurting you or isn't serving you.

Write five things you could let go of to find bigger healing.

Do: The Best You Can

Everyone's experience and level of depression are different. Some people are highly functioning depressives, while others can't get out of bed without crying.

There's no one face to depression. It's an equal opportunity employer. It doesn't care about skin color, income, sex, gender, or follower count. There is no right or wrong way to be depressed.

Depression is not always the sad image of someone sulking in a corner. It's Robin Williams, Anthony Bourdain, and Chris Cornell.

I don't know where you are at, but just do the best you can. Celebrate the momentum and steps you take. If you make a mistake don't punish yourself. Practice championing yourself.

You have a beautiful, magnificent life path, and it's so unique it's unlike any other person's on the planet. Meet yourself where you are at. Celebrate what you can do instead of what you can't. Every day a little bit of action is enough. Start small with implementing change and work from there.

Coda: Depression Is Like Getting Sober

The closest analogy I can think to compare depression to is getting sober. The question, what does it take for someone to come out of depression, is like asking, what does it take for someone to get sober?

The answer is different for every person because, just like sobriety, no two people's experiences of depression and healing are the same. Similar maybe, but not the same. The events, actions, and situations it takes to get to that point are unique and different for everyone. There is a necessity to hit bottom, and then you can't unsee what you just saw.

The truth of it is, when enough is enough, enough is enough. When you're ready, you're ready. Sometimes it takes five stints in rehab to get sober. Sometimes it's a gentle talk with a loved one. Some stories are drastic, near-death experiences, traumatic and heavy, and some are banal, ordinary, and unsexy. Some hit like lighting and are instant changes, while others are slow grinds seemingly filled with steps forward, backward, and sideways with enough volatility to make the 2020 stock market seem tame.

I do believe that the moment you finally hit bottom and admit you need help is the exact moment when the universe starts working for you, and that's when the real healing begins. It can be a hard and bumpy road getting to that point. Be kind to yourself if you're not where you want to be.

Ultimately, I think it comes down to this: We are all on our own path. We all wake up in our own time. When you are ready to wake up, you will wake up. I believe with every cell of my being, there is no such thing as being late to our own healing. I believe that whatever we do, we are always on our path, and we are always on time. Again, you're ready when you are ready. You are exactly where you need to be.

Chapter Three:

DEPRESSION 101
Depression for Dummies

The closest thing to a divorce I've had was when my professional rock band of eight years fell apart. I used to joke that being in a rock band was like being married to four guys; everything was my fault, I was financially responsible for everything, and the sex was nonexistent. I didn't even get a blowjob. When the band did eventually fall apart, the universe dragged me through the full extent of this joke's ridiculousness.

One member demanded fifty thousand dollars and falsely claimed writing credit on songs he never wrote. Another member went off the deep end and became convinced I had been harboring a murder plot against him for six years. Another tried to steal my equipment and refused to move out of my parents' house, which resulted in a near Wild West standoff between him and my mom. One left for a bigger, flashier band. One got canceled online. One I never talked to again, like we never met. The only thing I knew was that, after this, I never wanted to be in a rock band ever again.

Behind the shock, anger, and confusion of the fallout was something I wasn't willing to admit to myself: pure heartbreak of the highest order. The thing I'd put my entire life, being, identity, and all of my focus into ended abruptly and without my acceptance or consent. I felt like I'd lost my purpose, lost brothers, and I was not awake enough to fully mourn that or realize the magnitude of what I was moving through.

When it ended, I had no direction for my life, and the only inkling of guidance I had was my inner voice telling me to move back home with my family in Santa Barbara, buy a bunch of recording gear, and make a record at home.

So I bought the gear, set it up, and started working. At that point, I'd been writing and recording for years. I was pretty good at it, but this time something was off.

This time, it was hard. Not the normal difficult like learning a new skill, but ten times as hard as it should have been.

I felt like I was out of focus all the time. I couldn't think straight, couldn't understand what any of the gear did, and couldn't focus on making anything cohesive. Stringing thoughts together in a clear, rational way, or accessing any sort of depth, felt impossible.

I used to be able to write full songs in thirty minutes, and now it was taking me three hours to write a single verse without lyrics. In addition to that, I was still knee-deep in depression.

It was also difficult to focus on the sound of a high hat, or the second verse lyric, when fifteen minutes in, my brain would chime in and landslide me with depressive thoughts. All these ideas are terrible; you wrecked your life beyond repair; you might as well go kill yourself. I was still in denial about my depression, but at that point I didn't realize my depression was bottoming out.

I managed to slog through and finish the record.

It wasn't until years later that I fully understood what had happened. I had started taking antidepressants and seeing a therapist. One day I was in her office telling her something really weird was happening from taking antidepressants.

For the first time in over ten years, I was actually able to think clearly. It was bizarre. I was writing songs and able to think deeply and focus on things like language and melody. I was able to access deep thought and be a participant in life.

She looked about as surprised as if I had just told her that boys have penises. She said, "That makes sense because brain fog, the inability to think clearly, is a symptom of depression. It's like you've been on drugs for a decade, and your brain is finally working again."

I went mute out of shock and almost cried. I felt so

stupid. How the hell could I have not known that brain fog was a symptom of depression?

I looked back on my entire twenties and realized, Christ, I've been working with a broken brain. I looked back on all the time spent struggling to make a record and felt so dumb. I thought I knew what depression was, but it had been affecting me in ways I wasn't even aware of. I looked back on the decade of my life and asked, What other symptoms did I have, and what other ways had depression manifested without me being aware of it?

I want you to know everything you're up against. If we want to slay the beast, we need to know everything about it; how it works, how it moves, how it targets you. Knowing this is power, and it gives you the clarity and strength to make better choices. What I didn't know kept me suffering longer, and I don't want that for you.

This chapter is about the basics of depression. I want to lay out the map and clearly present all the ways a depressed brain works and how it can show up in your thoughts, belief systems, actions, and consciousness. This is all in hopes of shining the light of awareness so you can start to cultivate consciousness on the path you are taking with depression. When we know what we are up against, we have an easier time fighting it.

Symptoms of Depression

Here is a master list of potential symptoms of depression.

- A feeling of wanting to die, the desire to not exist, and thoughts of suicide.
- Isolation. Not wanting to be around anyone or talk to anyone. Retreating. A desire to disappear, become invisible.
- A dullness and numbness, a deadening of the senses. Inability to feel or access heart or gut/intuition space.
- Lack of joy, inability to play or allow yourself to explore, find wonder, and connectedness in this world.
- Losing interest in things that once brought you joy.
- A deep sense of unworthiness; feeling inferior, less than, and like something is deeply, fundamentally wrong with you while everyone else is ok. Thoughts like: "I don't deserve to be alive, or be happy, or achieve my dreams." Not living the life you want because of low self-worth.
- Deep persisting sadness and mourning for no clear reason. Wanting to cry all the time without cause or reason. Crying all the time.
- Feeling deeply separate from this world, feeling outside of life, not on the playing field of humanity. It's like being enclosed in a glass box, witnessing life but not a part of it. Life is happening all around you, but you don't feel "in it."

- A weight and heaviness to everything. Tightening and seriousness.
- Your energy is gone. You are drained, tired, fatigued, exhausted all the time.
- Everything is harder than it used to be. Things that were easy are now extremely difficult. Doing anything becomes a burden and requires twice as much energy as it once did. Everything feels forced. Going out is a burden. People and social interactions become terrifying, impossible, and immobilizing. Sometimes you can't get out of bed. No energy for even basic self-care, such as showers and eating.
- Being in mental pain or physical pain and anguish, most of your waking moments, and just wanting all of it to stop.
- Lack of hope and possibility. Feeling hopeless about your future. Excitement about plans is gone. Dreams, aspirations, goals, and hopes for your life disappear, and things feel impossible. Like being caught in a riptide and being under so long you forget there is light.
- Sleep patterns are off. Sleeping a lot, or not at all. Your sleep is terrible.
- Lack of clarity. Never feeling truly awake. Existing in a groggy brain fog, feeling off, dissociated, distracted, living in a dream, feeling like a camera lens is out of focus. Looking at life through a muddy windshield.

- Severe brain fog, inability to think clearly or with depth. Thinking in fragments; scattered, shallow thought patterns.
- Eating habits are changed. Eating is difficult or not appealing.
- Anxiety attacks, panic attacks. Intense fear, worrying, feeling of impending doom, pounding heart, racing and ruminating mind.
- Feeling in danger most of the day, like everything is a threat. You're in fight or flight 24/7.
- Feeling like a failure, with a strong proclivity to see the negative in everything.
- Making decisions based on fear, hopelessness, scarcity, and unworthiness instead of excitement, enthusiasm, and passion.
- The brain finds insult with everyone and everything; finding reason to feel wounded, victimized, down, and out.

What comes up for you as you read this list? Are any of these surprising or shocking for you? I wanted to include this list in case you're not fully aware of all the symptoms of your depression.

Reread this list. Identity what feels true for you. The power here is in awareness. These symptoms are a map. They tell us where to go and where we need work. When we can determine exactly how depression is making us feel, we can start to take action and heal those parts of us.

The Origins of Depression

My first introduction to spirituality was years ago when my friend Elaine bought me a copy of Autobiography of a Yogi by Yogananda. It's filled with mystical stories of Indian saints performing miracles. These ancient masters do wild shit—like one survived years on light alone (no food), another could be in two places at the same time, many could mind read, and some, by merely tapping their fingers, could knock another person into samadhi (the experience of universal bliss, oneness and merging with God).

At the time I read this, I remember thinking, there's no way any of this can be true. But then and I paused and thought, but what do I have to lose by believing these stories? This is what I'm asking you to do right now as we explore the question, where does depression come from?

The answer to this question inspires as many arguments and different responses as asking a New Yorker where the best slice of pizza is in the city. Depending on the lens through which we look at depression, the answer changes. Depression is as mystical as life, and in turn, its origins can be mysterious. Here are a few places depression could come from.

Chemical Imbalance or Genetics

It's possible that your depression could be an issue of chemical imbalance. This is the simple "Western medicine" answer. Your brain isn't producing enough chemicals; here are some pills, and now you are fixed. Looking at depression through this lens, we will usually only get information about neurology and chemicals.

This could absolutely be the case, but I think it is only part of the story. Why is there a chemical imbalance? When we only focus on chemicals or genetics, we aren't taking into account the bigger questions of our life or depression, like self-care, identity, existential crisis, purpose, and so on. I'll discuss all of these later. Depression is of mind, body, spirit, soul, ancestry, and trauma. Saying it's only of the mind or biology limits the scope of how we heal from depression.

I also think this answer can sometimes be a cop-out to avoid the actual inner work that needs to be done. There is something fundamentally sketchy and avoidant about "it's just my DNA!" or "Take these pills, you'll be better." It addresses the symptoms and not the root cause. A lot of people take antidepressants and are still depressed, and when we get to the antidepressants section I'll explain why.

Trauma

As a kid, it didn't take a lot to traumatize me. I was probably the most sensitive kid of all time, with a nervous system so fragile it could be sent into a panicked overdrive with a sudden glance. What really wrecked me above all else were monsters: Frankenstein especially.

In 1995, when I was five, my family went to see A Goofy Movie. No one could have envisioned that during the first five minutes of the opening sketch, a character would grotesquely morph into Frankenstein. It's no exaggeration to say that I didn't sleep for months because I was so traumatized.

I spoke to my close friend Dr. Courtnay Meletta about trauma. She is a stellar therapist, an even better person, and has been a mental health advisor for this book.

She said trauma is energy that is stuck in your body following an incident. Something happens, and your body and nervous system have a response and then hold onto that energy.

Note: It's more about how you respond to the event than the actual event. Two people can experience the same thing; one person is traumatized, the other is fine.

During and after trauma, our body creates stories that we internalize, like "I'm not safe," "I'm going to die," "The world isn't safe," or "I'm not worthy."

Trauma affects your belief system, which affects thoughts, which affects emotions and behavior patterns. It also shapes our nervous system and physiology to respond and experience life in particular ways until we heal it.

These beliefs and stuck energy can lead to depression. In this case, Courtnay offers a definition of depression as "stuck energy." Unprocessed trauma can wreck our lives in ways we aren't aware of, from attracting the wrong partners to addiction, to depression and anxiety, to feeling unworthy and shameful in every area of our life.

In this way, depression can be a symptom of trauma. Similar to my own depression and healing, Courtnay's definition suggests that depression can be a symptom of something else. Therefore, if we address underlying root trauma, our depression gets better. Later, we'll explore ways to do this.

Harkening back to my Goofy Movie fiasco, I was left traumatized with the belief that I'm not safe anywhere if Frankenstein is in a fucking Disney movie. That terror and lack of safety didn't leave my body for months; every night I was terrified to go to sleep. Other kids my age who saw that scene probably just laughed or thought that was awesome. Same event, different reactions.

To put it all together—unprocessed energy gets stuck in our body following an incident our systems experience as traumatic, which then leads to the creation of narratives and beliefs around our self and the world, which can then lead to depression. Trauma is also rooted in the nervous system, which detects threats and safety every millisecond of our lives from the time of birth (and likely in utero). One of the crazy things about trauma is it can be pre-language.

Birth trauma

I was born two months early and put in an incubator where I was without physical touch. As an adult, I would tell people this as a funny story, "I just couldn't wait to be alive, so I came out two months early at three pounds and twelve ounces." I later found out there was a sad truth to this.

During a medicine ceremony, I relived my experience of being a premature baby. I felt the pain and torture of being isolated and alone in the incubator. I felt the despair of being without touch. I felt my mom's anxiety at not being able to hold her newborn and her fear of not knowing if I'd make it. I felt dumb, panicked, and confused. This created stories like, Why is no one touching me? Why is no one helping me? Can't anyone see I'm suffering? What's wrong with me?

Running along this story, my entire existence, I have felt "outside of life" and separate from everyone. I've never felt like I belonged and never felt a part of this world (a symptom of depression). I never felt truly close to people. I never knew why until this ceremony.

The medicine told me all those beliefs and feelings had stemmed from the trauma of lack of touch as a premature baby.

When the ceremony ended, I was in disbelief. Could this actually be true?

A few months later, I met a child therapist and told her about my experience as a premature baby, and she validated everything.

The trauma of being without touch had instilled some belief in me of being separate, and as a result of this, I felt outside of life. This most likely contributed to my depression and feelings of isolation.

My point with this story is that our depression can stem from birth trauma: trauma from the womb or the birth process. We might not even remember or be conscious of this trauma, but it can still affect us.

If this wasn't wild enough, it turns out we can also hold trauma that isn't even ours.

Ancestral trauma

The idea of ancestral trauma is that we carry pain and trauma that is passed onto us by our ancestors. Our parents or grandparents had some sort of trauma and didn't deal with it, and now we are left to pay the bill for their suffering. It's a fascinating concept to think that the pain and suffering we experience might not even be ours.

Just like our receding hairlines, certain beliefs around wealth or well-being can be passed down from generation to generation. Depression, suicidal ideation, and thoughts like, I don't deserve to be alive, can seep into our being from our genetic lines.

We are energetic beings, and we live in an energetic universe. If you are sensitive (which most depressed people are), you can pick up on other people's energy, sometimes even absorbing it as your own. Some of these painful beliefs about yourself or depression might not even be yours. The DNA of both our parents and grandparents is still in us, so it makes sense that we could absorb our family's suffering and trauma.

Looking into our family history and what their belief systems and trauma are is a good way to start to heal. Seeing what's theirs and what is not ours.

As I walk on my own path, a lot of my work has been letting go of fear, unworthiness, and trauma that isn't mine. It's from my family. I find myself asking, Is this even mine? when I'm in situations and feeling a certain way that confuses me.

If holding onto your ancestors' trauma wasn't enough, it turns out we can be scarred from things that happened to us in a past life.

Past life trauma

I've had an obsession with death since I was a teenager, and I never felt a sense of safety around other people. In every room I walk in, I scan for danger. It turns out, as mushrooms told me, this stemmed from being murdered in a past life.

I relived a scene of hundreds or thousands of years ago of being a young Asian mother with a daughter of around five, hiding in a cart during a war. A soldier found us and immediately murdered both of us with his sword.

When this was revealed to me, it was like everything clicked and made sense. I felt both relieved and certain. I've had reoccurring nightmares of variations of this same scene, of being found and murdered, since I was a kid. When I saw the origin, it felt viscerally true. I've heard other people having unexplainable hardships in this life, and hearing of a past life regression helps make sense of it, and everything lands.

So we could be carrying depression as trauma from a different incarnation. Same soul, different incarnation. Something traumatic could have happened to us in a past life that scarred our soul, and we still carry that burden and weight.

Energy

This is the one I wish I was joking about, but I've heard too many firsthand accounts (including my own). You could have a demon, spirit, or entity riding with you in your body or in your home. If you feel this is the case, put down this book and hire an exorcist or energy healer.

Diving into the I-can't-believe-my-spiritual-path-is-getting-this-wacky folder, during the editing process of this book, my energy worker ex-girlfriend and a Russian shaman friend came to my parents' house to clear out the spirit of a murdered Chumash Indian.

She said the stuck, repressed energy of the spirit can affect everyone living in the house. Going back to the stuck energy notion, your depression can be stuck energy of other spirits or a place or house.

Spirituality

Your depression could stem from the big holy shit existential questions of being a human on this planet. The search for God, or feeling a lack thereof. Your depression might be constellated around a crisis of identity: What does it mean to be a tiny human on this big planet in a bigger universe? Depression can be rooted in disillusionment with life and society. It might be sourced from the pain and suffering of ignorance, of forgetting who we are and where we come from. This was where ninety percent of my suffering from depression came from.

Life Choices

Our personal life choices can also contribute to our depression. I call these the "manageables." These are the things in our life we can control through daily choices. Living in alignment, practicing self-care, dealing with our thoughts and beliefs, and finding the present moment can help us find peace. We're going to dive deep into this in the next few chapters.

A Big Life Change

Lastly, a big event, like the death of a loved one, a pandemic, a loss of any kind (job, relationship), or any kind of change, can send us into suffering.

As you read this list, read it lightly and don't get over-whelmed. We are going to dive deeper into a lot of these concepts as the book goes on. Don't be too obsessed with figuring out the root of your depression. It will be revealed to you at exactly the moment you're meant to know. Spending too much time needing to know why you are depressed is time taken away from handling and healing the actual depression and taking action. Just focus on taking steps right now to heal. Trust you'll know what you need to know when you need to know it.

To throw back to Chapter 1, no matter where your depression comes from, it doesn't negate the idea that it is a teacher here to bring you to the highest version of your-self. Your soul chose depression as its work in this lifetime. Depression is here to help your awakening. It's no mistake.

Mindsets of Depression

Depression is an ecosystem or matrix. It's a web or network of beliefs, mindsets, perceptions, thoughts, actions, and habits that all feed into each other. This changes the lens through which you see the world. Knowing how a depressed brain works is key to finding relief.

Even though it doesn't seem like it, a depressed brain is our friend. Our brain is not the enemy. It's an ally in our healing. It's trying to protect us and keep us safe. The prob-lem is, the way it "protects" us is in ways that don't work.

It uses a handful of low-level mindsets, frequencies, and closed-loop energies to keep us stuck. Again, these are all measures that our brain uses to keep us safe, but they just prolong our suffering. (These are our brain's own unhealthy coping mechanisms.) When we act from these places, they create more of the same. Anxiety leads to more anxiety. Pessimism attracts pessimism.

When we see the world and function from this place, our lives can quickly turn to ruin and block healing. I wanted to close out this chapter with some of the mindsets that support depression and can keep us stuck. If we are aware of this, we can start to get power over it. I'm not going to get into neurology, but I will discuss thought processes and patterns. We can't think our way out of depression with a depressed brain.

What follows are what I call the greatest hits of depression.

Greatest Hits of Depression

If depression were a greatest hits record, these would be the songs. If depression was Snow White, these would be the dwarves. If depression was a mob boss, these would be its capos and thugs. If depression were a language, this would be the alphabet. Ok, enough, you get it. These are the mindsets that depression can create, and these mindsets can create depression. They keep us stuck.

Greatest Hit #1: Pessimism and Hopelessness

When I was depressed, I joked that the glass wasn't half full or half empty, but it's been dropped and shattered on the ground and I stepped in it and my foot is bleeding everywhere, and now my nice pants have coffee stains on them.

Pessimism is the opposite of hope and possibility. You don't believe things will get better. You're unable to believe in positive outcomes for anything, including your own healing.

A depressed brain, by nature, is pessimistic, with notes of perfectionism. It's always scanning, looking for fault, blame, shame, failure, or other things to be unhappy about. You could get a ninety-nine percent on a test, and it's the one percent that you obsess about and ruminate endlessly over. You believe in the worst-case scenario for everything, and the kicker is, because of this, you attract worst-case scenarios.

The Way Out: Optimism

Listening to a depressed brain about the future is like hiring a fortune teller who tells you the apocalypse is coming every time you see her. There are so many positive outcomes for your life even though you are depressed and can't think of them. We just need to practice remembering that.

Anytime you catch yourself thinking negatively about the future, pause and write what the best-case scenario would be for that situation. If you have trouble with that, just imagine a better outcome than the one you are stuck on. Consistently flex your possibility muscles by taking small steps that shift what you think is possible. Keep reminding yourself the negative outcomes your brain thinks up aren't the truth or certain; they are just one small possibility in the infinite possibility of life.

Greatest Hit #2: Fear

Depression can make you afraid of everything—yourself, your thoughts, other people. This fear can lead to indecision and paralysis, which can keep you stuck, unable to flow with life, create stagnation and worsen your depression. Nothing in your life changes because you are too afraid to change anything.

The relationship you have with fear is the relationship you have with life. Try to see it as something of a guide, telling you what you can work on, and be brave. Fear is a teacher, just like depression. It's not a bad thing. It's trying to protect you against future painful outcomes.

One of my depression fears was about getting off anti-depressants. I thought I'd go right back into a place of being destitute and suicidal. It was my biggest fear. I forced myself to make the leap and get off them, and when I did, there was no problem at all. Fear is just one assumption in a universe of possible outcomes.

The Way Out: Trust

Acknowledge and befriend fear, listen to its wisdom, but never let it make your decisions. Fear and pessimism are similar in that they imagine worst-case scenarios. Practice taking small actions in the face of fear. In those situations, ask, what would the bravest version of myself say or do? We don't know how anything is going to be unless we show up there in the present moment.

Greatest Hit #3: Lack

This refers to focusing on everything you're not and everything you don't have. It's a classic recipe for suffering. Comparing yourself and your life path with others is a great way to let lack lead. Often with depression, we can focus on all the things we aren't, placing too much emphasis on what isn't here.

The Way Out: Gratitude

When we focus on what we don't have, we can't experience gratitude for what we have. We are only seeing what's missing instead of the beauty. Finding small things to be grateful for daily and really feeling into it—not just mindlessly writing a gratitude list, but finding one thing, like that you have eyes that can see—is a way out of lack.

Also, your life path is so unique it can't be compared with anyone else. No one else is like you. Don't compare your life, your path, your success, or your emotional state with anyone else's.

Greatest Hit #4: Victimhood

Being a victim is thinking the entire world has an agenda and is out to get you. When something goes wrong, it's always someone else's fault and never yours. Victims don't take responsibility for any of their actions or behavior. If you don't take responsibility, you don't grow or change. A person being a victim doesn't have the capacity to look inside of themselves and self-reflect. It's a fear pattern and a loop.

I want to note that there are real victims of crime, rape, and war, and this is not what I'm speaking about here. I'm speaking about a victim mindset; having tools and competency but still refusing to take responsibility for your life. It's lending out your power and efficacy.

The Way Out: Radical Responsibility

No one else is responsible for your depression and happiness but you. Take full and complete ownership of your mental health. No one else can heal you but yourself and the decisions you make. No one else is keeping you from healing.

We all need to take individual responsibility for our own health and happiness. Healing and happiness is an internal job. No one else can fill those holes inside of you, just like you can't fill other people's holes. Own your path, take full responsibility for your healing, and begin to take action.

Take responsibility for your side of the street. See where you can do better, looking at yourself with compassion, clarity, and honesty. What would you tell your best friend if s/he were in your situation?

Greatest Hit #5: Unworthiness and Shame

This is where you feel undeserving of life or of anything good happening in your life. Your mind attacks you with shame about who you are and the decisions you've made. Unworthiness and shame can cut off positive flow big time in areas like love, money, relationships, and jobs.

The Way Out: Affirmations

Whenever you catch yourself in a pattern of unworthiness or shame, replace it with an affirmation.

> I deserve to be happy and alive.
> I deserve to be free of depression.
> I deserve to live a beautiful and deep life.

Practice self-compassion. You are doing the best you can with the tools you have right now. Who and where you are right now is enough. You are worthy of life. The fact that you were born is proof enough. It's no mistake.

Greatest Hit #6: Rumination

Depression runs on loops. Your brain tells you the same negative stories about yourself, your life, and the world around you, over and over again. The danger is we have physical and emotional reactions to those stories, which keep giving life to those stories. We might even start to believe those stories.

The Way Out: Presence

I'm devoting a whole chapter to this later. We'll do a deep dive then!

Greatest Hit #7: Anger

I loved anger when I was depressed because it mobilized me in some way—even if that action was destroying my equipment on stage or scaring the hell out of my band members and crew with my rage. Anger isn't sustainable. It often causes us harm and leaves us with a hangover that takes a lot of repair. Behind anger is pain. It's usually fear.

The Way Out: Self-Compassion

Learning how to love ourselves and tend to our pain is the way to move through anger. Emotional release tools, like hitting or screaming into a pillow, can help move the energy of anger so we can get to the emotions beneath it.

Chapter Four:

SELF-CARE

Wisdom from a Haunted House

When I was nineteen, I made a ballsy bet with my parents. I was attending college and hated every second of it because I wanted to be a full-time musician. I begged them, "Please, let me take a semester off, give me six months to get a record deal, and if I don't by the end of the six months, I'll go back to school." They said yes.

I moved off campus and found a brand new one-bedroom cottage in Eagle Rock. It was adorable and shockingly affordable. The truth was, I couldn't have picked a more sinister hellhole to live in.

The morning I moved in, a visibly wasted neighbor saw me unloading music equipment and came wobbling down the street to say hi. He was in his thirties, living at home, and at 9 a.m., he brought over his vodka bottle to offer his new neighbor a shot. Through his slurring, I heard my least favorite phrase of all time, "We should jam sometime." But what bothered me more was something he said about the house.

"You didn't look this place up on Google Maps yet?" he said, like it was as obvious as not using a condom twice.

When he left, I ran to my computer, looked up the house, and saw on Google Maps that the house in which I stood was no house at all but instead charred ruins.

Another neighbor later that day told me the history of the house. Two brothers lived next door to each other, one in this house and one in the next. In Breaking Bad fashion, they started a side hustle and created a meth lab in the garage next door.

It went about as well as a meth lab can go. One brother's wife and kids left him and he was fired from his job because apparently he used the meth rather than sold it.

One day a fire broke out in the lab, burning down both houses, killing one brother, and leaving the other homeless and alone. He still wandered the area and often tried to get into the house, for which I had just signed a twelve-month lease.

The thing I didn't realize at first about the place was that the energy was bad. Like sinister bad. Like pissed-off spirits still lived there and were hell-bent on causing a ruckus with whoever came close.

Some examples: My bass player and girlfriend both had agonizing experiences of encountering ghosts in the house and never wanted to come over again. I experienced sleep paralysis, during which I saw a demon entity from the underworld writing on the wall. I had friends who walked in and immediately walked out because of the terrible vibes.

I was already beginning to struggle with depression in college, and when I moved into this cottage, it was like the cottage saw my energy and said, "Hold my drink."

Within weeks I fell apart. This cute cottage became the backdrop of my first major depressive episode.

I felt like I was nineteen going on ninety-five. I felt like life had nothing left to offer me. All I cared about and thought about was death. I became obsessed with the afterlife and what's next. I started going to graveyards four times a week. Depression and anxiety were hitting hard, and at that point in my life, I had no idea what depression or anxiety was. No one ever explained it to me. I spent a lot of time just hoping I'd get hit by a bus or knocked into a coma and finally be out of this pain and the burden that was existence.

At the time, I had no self-care routines. I was so lost in the unworthiness trance of depression that it never occurred to me to take care of myself. So when depression came, it took me down without a fight.

My diet was terrible: All I ate was fried food, a lot of processed meat, and truckloads of sugar. I was making black tea as strong as cocaine and hitting it all day long.

My sleep schedule was a disaster. I was often not sleeping enough or at all because of the caffeine.

I had no set schedule or anything to ground me. Between panic attacks, I'd write songs around midnight and would stay up until 3 or 4 a.m., waking up at 8 or 9 to do it all over again.

I wasn't working out.

I didn't have any kind of faith or spirituality to ground me or get me through.

My place was always a disaster. Dirty clothes and dishes were everywhere. When I left for my first tour, I left a massive pile of dishes in the sink. I returned three weeks later to a mountain of mold.

I was basically raw-dogging depression with no coping tools at all.

This hell lasted six months, which felt like two years. Unbelievably, at the end of those six months in which my life and mental state plummeted down into the abyss, I'd somehow managed to find a manager, band, and sign a record deal. Now it was time to learn how to be a rock star and make records.

This chapter about self-care might be both the most unsexy chapter and the most important. I boldly and firmly assert that if you don't implement the self-care measures that follow, you might as well put this book down and give depression your life and throne. This chapter is about taking care of your physical body.

When we take care of our physical body, it becomes a lot easier to take care of our mental, emotional, and spiritual bodies. When we lose self-care, it gives depression an open field to run wild. Maintenance and proper self-care are the foundation upon which the other practices and shifts in this book will build.

The most important relationship we will ever have in our lives is with ourselves.

Self-care essentially asks the question, what is the relationship you have with yourself?

We can have everything in the world, but if we don't like and love ourselves, it's meaningless.

I'm going to present basic suggestions on how to take better care of yourself and your mental health. I'm asking you to look at these ideas, examine and question your relationships with them, and create intentions around these certain areas in your life. Be open. Try it. See if you feel better.

Does This Even Matter? What's the Point?

A short while after busting out of the hellhole cottage, I went to the doctor for a checkup and told her I was having a hard time with depression. Her quick answer was to eat healthy, exercise, watch Joel Osteen, and meditate. It felt like the biggest "fuck you" ever.

I want to die all the time, and you're telling me to eat kale, buy a Peloton, and watch a TV minister? Don't you understand the sheer fucking terror and pain I'm in 24/7? How the hell is Joel Osteen going to help me? I'm in an existential nightmare.

I didn't feel seen at all because she didn't understand the depth of existential hopelessness I was in. How the hell was eating vegetables going to help me?

What she told me felt like the same heartless and cold checklist advice you find online from psychologists, therapists, and doctors. "Seek out community, exercise ..."

If you're feeling this right now, too, I get it.

Looking back, the truth is, my doctor was right. All of those things matter. They do work. Sometimes they are only part of the story, though.

Self-care and maintenance are important because they set the stage and clear out the energy so we can accept bigger healing and do deeper work. If healing is a triangle, self-care is the bottom.

Self-care measures might not be an end-all for your depression, but these are the initial steps that set you up for the win later, the steps that make all the mindfulness and conscious work that much easier.

Self-care creates the runway you can land your plane on. It's the foundation, the cornerstone. Self-care is the guy that kneels and holds the football so you can kick it into the goal for a win.

Proper self-care can mellow out the harshness, even out the lows, and give you a leg up in fighting depression and anxiety. It's the work we think is unsexy, but it's honestly the work that affects how you show up in every area of your life.

From the story I told above, I don't think my depression

would have been nearly as bad if I had had the tools to take better care of myself and observed basic maintenance and self-care.

A contractor friend of mine says that little leaks can cause big problems. This chapter is about those leaks.

Gumbo

In regards to self-care, you are like a pot of gumbo. If something is added to the pot, it affects the entire soup. If we add something that shouldn't be there or an ingredient is missing, it affects everything else.

What I'm saying is you are an ecosystem. What you eat, how you move, when you sleep, the information you consume, and the actions you take directly affect your moods, emotions, feelings, mental health, and spirituality. Everything affects everything else. Everything matters.

For example, for me, sleep and mental health are interwoven. If I don't sleep, I go crazy. When I don't sleep, I not only feel physically terrible, but it makes it nearly impossible for me to meditate or think straight. Lack of sleep shreds my presence, which then affects my decision-making and moods. Because I'm not thinking clearly, it lowers my defenses, which makes it easier for anxiety and depression to sneak in, and before I know it, I'm on the floor in the fetal position, crying about a mirage of a problem I'll most likely never have to solve.

By the same token, if you're getting high or drunk out of your mind, it can leave you depleted, making it harder to access gratitude or the proper consciousness and mindsets to tune into God and possibility. Your power here lies in the choice of what you let in and what you leave out of your life.

In a way, you can see every aspect of self-care as an issue of mental health. The way you use your phone affects your mental health, what you eat affects your mental health, and so on. We can begin to see everything in our lives as either serving our mental health or not.

It's All Energy, Man

Everything in this universe is energy and vibration. Every emotion has a frequency. People, places, even plants have frequencies. These frequencies can be high or low, light or heavy, fast or slow. You are a vibration right now, emitting a frequency.

Ever walk into a room after a couple has been screaming at each other? It's a very different energy than two hundred people praying and meditating together in an ancient church.

The vibration and energy of depression can feel stuck, heavy, and slow.

Compare that to being fully in gratitude, an energy that feels light, blissful, clear, and selfless.

We can only be and exist in one frequency at a time. We can't be in anger and gratitude at the same time. We are never static. We are continually in a dance between different feelings and emotions. When we start to tune into this, we can start to feel the difference.

Going back to the gumbo analogy, everything we do and interact with affects our frequency and vibration.

Consider that all these forms of self-care and maintenance are ways of shifting your own energy and being. Eating right, sleeping well, and exercising are ways of raising your vibration out of depression, so you can get out of the fog and begin to rewrite the story of your life.

Whenever I feel stuck or tired, I practice fifteen to twenty minutes of yoga, and I feel like a different person. It's a totally different vibe than if I just mindlessly scroll on Instagram.

We can't change our depression from the same frequencies that created it. Adding more anxiety, fear, pessimism, and lack to what's already there won't pull us out. We have to reach and aim higher. Love, gratitude, service, selflessness, awe, hope, trust, and presence are the ones we reach for that will guide us out of it, and self-care is the key to helping us support that.

Energies also attract like energies. Frequencies attract like frequencies. It's why that hellhole of a cottage was like a nest for me to have my depressive episode. Surround yourself with low energy, and you start to attract low-energy things.

Start to dance with higher energies, and you'll start to raise your vibration.

A Gift Not a Burden

We all have this weird and beautiful responsibility as human beings given these mystical bodies. We are their protectors and wardens. Our bodies are sacred physical vessels and vehicles for our consciousness, soul, and spirit. This is a big deal. We forget it's a privilege, not an obligation, to keep them running. Providing for them should be a gift—a nourishing and nurturing experience, not a 24/7 panic attack.

You are precious cargo. Your life, your body, your mind, and your spirit make up a beautiful garden that needs to be tended with love, care, compassion, and admiration.

Unfortunately, given the way we are raised, we are usually at war with ourselves mentally and physically, hating our bodies, not taking care of ourselves. We are mostly taught to think we aren't enough; aren't fit, or tall, or handsome enough, and so on.

When we deprive ourselves of basic maintenance, we give depression and anxiety an open field to run rampant.

Often we forget that our body has more intelligence than our brains. Instead of learning how to tune in and pausing to listen to it, we let our minds and fear rule and take on unhealthy habits that we think will help us.

Give yourself the dignity of holding yourself like something to be taken great care of, like a precious gem. See this self-care as a wonderful and intimate way of getting to know yourself better. You can take care of what you need.

I don't want these to feel like chores. Something like exercising your body is a gift and a celebration of being. The secret to all of this is exploring your relationship with it and making it fun.

If any of this feels like a chore, change the story behind it or change your actual approach. Find a way of eating, sleeping, and exercising that you love. Keep flipping the script of how you see them and the relationship you have with them until you feel excited and motivated to do it daily. See what you have to gain instead of what you have to lose.

Find the reframe for you. I couldn't break my social media addiction until I saw it through the lens of being a spiritual issue and one of consciousness. It was taking me out of presence and keeping me away from God because it was wrecking my moods and self-worth. Explore and experiment. Do whatever works for you.

Self-care is a wonderful journey of getting to know yourself. It's about exploration and discovery, not damnation and dictatorship. Learn about how you function, what nourishes you, what helps you, and what doesn't help you. It's all part of the path to healing.

Here is a brief list of self-care paths to explore to clean out your life inside and out.

House and Possession Cleanup

I have a home recording studio, and when my mental health was at its worst, gear was piled to the ceiling. The room could have been featured on Hoarders: Buried Alive. Dust-covered guitar amps, dozens of guitars, stacks of keyboards, and other broken and vintage miscellaneous music equipment. The joke was I didn't even use most of that gear.

At the time, I was making a record alone, and depression left me unable to think. Here I was, piled in a room where I was tripping on cables and outboard gear in a chaotic mess. I was having a mental breakdown, and my physical spaces mirrored that.

Our physical spaces are a representation of our mental health. Our mental health shows up in ways far beyond our thoughts—what we own, what we hold onto, and how we decorate and arrange our living spaces are no exception. Cluttered room = cluttered mind. Let go of anything that doesn't bring joy or make you happy. Old clothes, photos, shabby things; let them all go.

Remember, it's all energy. Being in a messy, dirty room cluttered with things you don't like, want, or need creates stuck energy. If you're piled to the ceiling with possessions, it's usually fear and hoarding energy. Let it all go. Open up the flow. This matters big time, and the changes you make will make a huge difference.

Take a look at your living space. Is it dirty? Clean? Do you even like what you see or what you own? Take a total inventory of everything you own. Begin the process of letting go of anything you don't need. Make your living space, however large or small, a sanctuary. Make it neat and clean.

Know where everything is. Open up the windows and let sunlight and air in. Sage your living space. Plants are great for changing energy.

If you're holding onto something, ask yourself why. Marie Kondo's The Life-Changing Magic of Tidying Up is a brilliant book to help you start this journey. The Minimalist documentary is also a great place to go for inspiration. Start small. Get rid of one thing a day.

When my mental health began to clear up, I began cleaning and discarding. I sold almost eighty percent of my music gear, and as soon as that happened, I actually began making the records I've always wanted to make.

It makes a huge difference. Try it.

Integrate:

> Look at your physical space and start discarding and making changes to it. Let your gut and intuition lead as you let go of possessions that don't serve you.

Morning Routine

I have two kinds of days: days when I do a morning routine and days when I don't. On days when I keep my morning routine, I feel focused, present, and calm. On days when I neglect my morning routine, I'm usually sprawled out on the floor, weeping.

A morning routine is a set series of practices that ground you and set you up for the win during the day. Meditation, morning pages (writing three pages freehand), exercising, not checking your phone or email before a certain time, and prayer are examples of morning routine practices.

How we spend the first hour of our day sets the mood for the day. For our mental health, meditating and exercising in the morning is a lot different than slamming eight coffees and doom-scrolling Instagram.

My own morning routine offers me presence and helps me reconnect with my purpose and spirit. When I skip it, I feel ungrounded, and I am more likely to fall prey to depression and its narratives. Having a morning routine ensures that you set the pace for the day and the day is not imposing on you.

Waking up at the same time and having the same routine every day is an incredible way to protect your mental health and set you up in a good way for the day.

Integrate:

Curate a morning routine that feels good for you. Give yourself time to experiment with what resonates with you and serves you.

Exercise

The last tour I did with my band was the most stressful thing I'd ever done. In two months, I went through three drummers and two bassists. Trying to organize simple things like a photoshoot or band practice felt like trying to seduce the Pope. It felt like everything I worked toward was falling apart while I was also dealing with my own mental health issues.

A girl I was dating at the time was into yoga, so in an attempt to woo her, I bought a Groupon for a yoga class. It saved my life. In my first class, I showed up in a bathing suit and knee-high socks. I had absolutely no idea what I was doing, but I did know it was the only hour of the day when I had some sort of respite from the suffering I was in.

Exercise is mandatory for better mental health. It moves static and blocked energy in our body and helps us feel better. It releases endorphins. It gets us out of our heads and into our bodies, bringing us back to the present moment.

Exercise can feel like a chore, especially when you don't have energy or you're feeling low. The best advice I have is to find something that lights you up.

I'm sure whatever city you live in has gyms offering free first-time classes or cheap passes for a week or month. Try different studios and different ways of working out. Try boxing, try yoga, try running, try all of it. Again, depression is about exploration, and it's a journey of finding yourself. Try whatever you can to see what really brings you joy and see what doesn't serve you. Make it a game. When something doesn't serve you, just move on and find something new.

I'd recommend working out four to five times a week. If you can't do something intense or prolonged, just take a walk or go outside in nature. The most important part is to just MOVE.

Integrate:

Make a plan to try different workout routines. Make it fun. Move your body four to five times a week.

Eating

It never occurred to me that diet could have anything to do with mental health. I would slam eight cups of coffee a day and then have Biblical-sized panic attacks. When I stopped drinking caffeine before a ceremony and my anxiety levels dropped, I paused and thought, dear God what have I been doing to myself?

What is your relationship with food? Food can heal you or hurt you. It can make us physically and mentally sick or set us free. It depends on the relationship you have with it.

Food, diet, and how you eat affect mood and mental health in a big way.

Food is energy. Food is vibration. Fruits and vegetables have different qualities of nourishment than processed fast food. Your body is sacred, and what you put in it should reflect that.

The energy of whatever we eat is transferred into our bodies. This is an argument vegans make; if a cow is terrified when it's killed, that fear energy is put into the meat, which your body digests. In the same way, highly processed food doesn't have that much nutrition or energy value.

What you eat

I can't really give blanket advice about what you should eat because every body is different and needs different things, but I'd recommend eating as naturally as you can. Cut out or limit artificial foods, soda, factory-farmed meat, fast foods, sugar, and caffeine. Eat mostly plants and foods that are nutritious and fuel your body.

Often we're pouring so much sugar, caffeine, and chemicals into our body we have no idea how we're feeling. When we're numbed or frazzled, accessing any sort of deep inner truth, wisdom, or guidance is impossible because we are constantly dealing with the physical pain of over- or under-eating or eating food that prevents our bodies from functioning well.

Mainly notice how you feel after you consume certain foods and drinks. Every body is different, and every body has different needs. You need to listen to your body and let it tell you what it needs.

An elimination diet can be helpful. You start taking out foods one by one, noticing how you feel, and then reintroducing them and noticing how you feel. You might keep a journal to track your experiences.

Notice when you crave certain foods or tastes, such as sugar or caffeine. Is it when you need an energy boost? Is rest the answer, or the actual substance?

How you eat

My friend Sasha is an Ayurvedic specialist, and she blew my mind one day. She said how we eat is just as important as what we eat.

How often do you eat? Is it three meals a day? Are they grounded meals? Are you sitting down and being present with what you're eating, or are you frantic and rushed?

As she suggests, treat your meals like you're taking yourself on the most romantic date of your life. Practice mindful eating. Take ten slow, conscious breaths before your meal. This calms your nervous system down and tells you it's time to eat. Pause before you eat to say gratitude. Chew fifty times per bite so you digest your food well. Take away all screens when you eat. No scrolling. Focus on the taste of the food. Notice the flavors and textures. Be present to actually experience it.

If we eat in a state of anxiety, our body is in fight-or-flight, and we can't properly digest food. In this state, eating can hurt our stomachs or cause discomfort and pain that affects our digestion.

Integrate:

Notice how you feel after you eat certain foods. Try eliminating certain foods from your diet and notice how it affects your mental health.

Practice mindful eating as mentioned above in the How You Eat section.

Alcohol and Drugs

After my band broke up, I started having panic attacks at night. They were so physically painful, it felt like a giant was stepping on my chest and cracking it open. Then I felt a space in my heart as wide as the Grand Canyon, which my entire spirit and body were sinking into at warp speed. Going to sleep became a cause for anxiety because of these panic attacks. I could distract myself all day, but being in bed was the only time I was alone with my thoughts.

I coped with weed. It felt like a miracle cure. I'd just take two hits from the vape and would be knocked into gentle oblivion. I thought I solved the problem until I realized it was actually solving nothing. I was in a classic addict cycle. I would wake up hungover as hell from the vape, and it would take hours of effort to pull myself out of it, only to get to another night and numb out with weed to escape the terror.

Yet, for a period of time, the weed saved my life. It helped turn down the brutal voice in my head. It kept me in a sort of holding pattern and alive long enough to find true healing. Then I hit a point where I realized it wasn't helping me long-term and knew I had to find a better way. The weed ultimately didn't fix the root of my anxiety. It just softened and numbed the symptoms.

If you drink or do drugs, I recommend stopping for a month. See how it affects your life, your body, and your depression.

Ask yourself: What is my relationship with these substances, and when and why do I use them? What's the reason behind why I drink? Am I using these substances to mask or heal?

There's always a reason behind the things we do. Some sort of hidden motive or intention. We most often don't drink wine or coffee because it tastes good. We drink for a reason. Because we need energy, we need to be "on" or take the edge off.

Is there a hidden intention? An "I don't want to feel this pain, and it's easier for me to get high and drink so I don't feel it" underlying motivation around your substance use? Are you trying to relieve the symptom or dig down to the root cause of why you are drinking?

Also, ask yourself honestly, how are these substances serving you? Do these substances make your life better? Are they really helping you, or are they hiding something? Do they expand consciousness or bludgeon it? Are they bringing you into confusion or clarity? Yes, the fun stories about how drunk you got last weekend are great, but are they just sarcasm hiding suffering, or a sad cry for something else? How do you feel after? Shame? Fear?

If you're using substances to cope right now, don't beat yourself up or hold judgment. We all do the best we can with the tools we have. When we are taught a better way, we adopt a better way. If drinking and getting high are the only coping tools you have right now, that's a-ok. You're doing the best you can. Maybe you don't know there are other options because no one told you.

If we're trying to cover something up or not feel something, the best way to heal is to feel it and face it head-on, not run through hoops of denial and hell loops. When you aren't willing to face the core reason—what's really going on, the underlying reason you are getting high or drinking—then you get stuck in a loop. The joke is this keeps us in a cycle. We are not alright without it. When we are under the influence of alcohol or drugs, we don't make positive changes in those states. All of this goes back to the First Steps rule about not running. (These ideas could be used for any addiction, social media, food, etc.)

Also, you either have a problem with alcohol and drugs, or you don't. You're an addict, or you're not. Some people can drink half a glass of wine and walk away from the restaurant with it unfinished. Some people drink a glass of wine and their brain chirps in, "Yes, this is good, but two bottles would be better."

If you have a problem or think you are an addict, seeking help is the best option. Alcoholics Anonymous (AA), Narcotics Anonymous (NA), therapy, or plant medicine can help. These support systems may help you discover the real reasons you drink or do drugs and address the previously buried and numbed feelings that you aren't willing to feel.

Even one glass of wine can affect your sleep, your clarity of thinking, your moods, and your mental health. It's a serious depressant. (Side note: I can't believe alcohol is legal and a societal norm. It's poison. Plus, the emotional aftermath of time, money, and hangovers you have to nurse and the emotional hell you put yourself through, beating yourself up about never drinking again. And so on. Crazy.)

Give it up for a month and see how it goes. If that is too hard, give yourself a smaller period of time to start and take it slow. Take it on a day-to-day basis if needed.

Integrate:

Stop drinking and doing drugs for a month. If this is too much, try a week or even a day or two.

If you think you have a problem with substance abuse, attend an AA meeting.

Antidepressants

Swallowing my first antidepressant felt like the greatest failure and betrayal of my life because I had so many stories around them. As an artist, I thought antidepressants would destroy my creativity and capacity to feel. My art wouldn't be "real." I felt ashamed of needing pills. I thought there was something unhealthy, unnatural, or unclean about it. It felt like cheating.

The bigger joke I couldn't see was that depression had already made all my worst fears come true. I already had no energy to create. I wasn't writing songs. I couldn't feel anything.

When I started antidepressants, I started playing and writing again with a level of depth I hadn't accessed for years. Joy came back.

The pills were like anesthesia; they quieted down the negative voices so I could access the energy, clarity, and focus to begin doing the work on my belief system, thoughts, and depression to find healing. They allowed me to do surgery on myself. They were the kick I needed to learn new skills and ways of coping. Within weeks I was able to function in life again.

Antidepressants don't do all the work for you. They don't magically fix your broken belief systems or self-worth problems, give you a purpose-filled life, or build your trust and faith in the universe. They can give you the lift and the space to do that, though. There are plenty of people who take antidepressants and are still depressed, and I think it's because they expect the pills to do all the heavy lifting. Antidepressants are best when paired with things such as therapy, shadow, trauma, and belief work.

The only drawback is it could take months to feel the full effects of antidepressants. Every body is different, and the medication will effect everyone in different ways. Sometimes, it can take up to six months to actually know how these pills work in your body or if they will even help. Sometimes you have weird side effects and have to switch pills. But could any of this be worse than your depression now? I thought I didn't have time to wait three months to see how the pill would affect me, so I spent six more years getting hammered by depression.

Antidepressants mystically left my life as quickly and unexpectedly as they came into my life. Six months in, I realized I'd hit my peak with them. I could tell my life wasn't going to change in a big way. I made the terrifying decision to get off them to do Ayahuasca, and I haven't been depressed a day since or needed pills.

It's no one's business what you do with your body and what medication you're on. It's a decision you have to make for yourself, and only you can say if it's right for you. I think they are just another tool in the toolkit that can serve you.

Integrate:

If you feel called to try antidepressants, make an appointment with a doctor you trust and talk to them about medication options.

1. Pair this with work with a therapist and inner work on your belief system, thoughts, and meditation.

Content Consumption

Many people in spiritual communities love crystals. During rituals and ceremonies, they put crystals on altars to "charge" them. This means the crystal absorbs the healing energy of the room, which can then be taken to other places and bless the new space with its presence.

I didn't fully understand how this worked until I turned into a crystal one night.

I had recently begun playing music at Ayahuasca ceremonies and acting as a helper/guardian. Helpers drink a tiny dose of medicine to tap into the flow of the room. When I did, the medicine turned me into a crystal and showed me that people are like crystals. Whatever we consume is absorbed into our being. Everything we expose ourselves to has an effect on us, which either brings us to light or weighs us down.

When we watch a violent movie or play a horror video game, our bodies don't know the difference between reality and fiction. When we die in a video game, it can trick our bodies and brain into thinking we are actually dying. When we watch a murder on screen, we might feel the same shock and horror as if it was happening to us. This is both the magic and curse of entertainment and media content.

If we watch things that make us feel awful (I'm guilty of binging shows like Black Mirror and Ozark that make me feel absolutely devastated after), we get physically and energetically infused with those vibes, which can affect our mental health. Binging news on the internet, TV, or radio can expose us to all that's going wrong in the world, and we can pick up on those negative vibrations.

Whatever energy and actions we fill ourselves with is what we radiate. Pay attention to what you consume and how you feel after.

Integrate:

Write down a list of all the entertainment, websites, news, and TV you consume. After your time with it, notice your body and mental state. How do you feel after you consume it?

Practice taking a week off from certain entertainment modalities —TV, news, social media—notice how it affects your mental health.

Social Media

Nothing has made me feel more terrible about myself, my worth, and my life on a more consistent basis than social media. I've bitched to my therapist more times than I would like to admit about how awful I feel about myself after using social media.

When I go on social media, I begin to unconsciously play the comparison game. I start comparing my life with other people's lives. I'm not as fit, I'm not as hot, I'm not as famous, I don't have as many followers, that guy's hairline is way better than mine. I always feel less than and awful, and I spiral out.

This sends me straight into lack. I'm not enough, I don't have enough, I'm not famous enough, and the big one, I don't matter. Then pessimism catches it, and I freak out. What if I never have those things? I'm a failure, I should go kill myself. Social media can destroy our mental health.

Ask yourself: How is social media contributing to your well-being? What is your relationship with it? How do you feel after you use it? Do you get your sense of self or worth from social media? Is it making you happy? Or making you anxious and miserable all the time? If it's the latter, change something.

Most importantly, when do you reach for it? Are you trying to use it as a pacifier? Trying to avoid something? I reach for it as a distraction when I don't want to feel something.

On a more sinister level, big corporations and tech are behind social media. They steal and sell our attention using every psychology trick in the book to keep you as addicted as possible. It's vicious. I love and hate it. It's been a beautiful connection vehicle for me and my music fans but also wrecked my emotional well-being.

Take responsibility for your relationship with social media. Set boundaries. Take a day off. Set certain times you can go on social media or not. What I'd really recommend, however, is taking a big break. Try a month without it. See how it affects your mental health. See how it affects your ability to think and be present and your moods.

Can you use social media in a way that doesn't affect your self-worth? Can you actually champion other people's lives instead of comparing yourself in a negative way? Seeing what other people are doing all the time and comparing yourself is a doom slide and the quickest way to suffering and depression.

Our phone is just a tool. We're not meant to have a hammer on us 24/7. Just like that, we don't need to be on social media or check things every minute of every day.

I see social media and phones as an issue of consciousness and spirituality. From a consciousness standpoint, it's breaking our brains, destroying our ability to concentrate and do deep work, and it's an addiction. It became a spiritual issue for me because it was destroying my consciousness and keeping me asleep. I was putting out the fires of lack and insecurity instead of being grounded in the present moment.

Unfollow everyone that doesn't bring you joy. Ask yourself the reason you follow people. We all have friends we feel obligated to follow whose feeds drain us. Mute or unfollow.

Integrate:

> Batch social media time. Set an allotted time of day
> to scroll (e.g., don't check social media before noon,
> or only check between 4–4:30, or only check emails
> the last ten minutes of every hour).
>
> Notice when and why you reach for your phone.
> What's the motivation behind why you scroll or
> why you want to post?
>
> As mentioned before, take a break (a week, a day, a
> month) and see how it affects your mental health.

Nighttime Routine

A nighttime routine is essentially the same thing as a morning routine except, you guessed it, it's at night. A nighttime routine is what you do to prepare for sleep and reflect on your day.

Reduce stimulation before bedtime

Be mindful of what sort of content you consume at night.

I'd recommend having no screens and no electronics in bed or in the bedroom. No watching movies in bed and no phones in bed. Also no TV screens or video games late at night. The only thing you do in bed is sleep and make love.

I practice a technology cutoff time every night. My cutoff time is usually 8 p.m. After that, I don't use social media, browse the internet, check emails or texts, and usually I don't take calls.

I do this because I know my body and myself. If I start scrolling on Instagram too late at night, I'll crash down the comparison slide and start to suffer and have panic attacks about my life. That's not the energy I want to give into before I go to bed.

The blue light from our phones messes with our circadian rhythms by tricking our eyes into thinking it's daytime, making it harder to fall asleep.

Whenever I break my no-tech nighttime rules, I am reminded almost immediately when I am wide awake in bed, having anxiety, why I set those rules in place.

In addition to limiting tech, you also want to consider limiting food before sleep. No eating two hours before you go to sleep—also, be mindful of sugar intake and what you eat before bed.

Nighttime ritual

Create a nighttime wind-down ritual. Make going to sleep something sacred. Treat going to sleep like a ceremony. Have a set series of habits, rituals, and patterns that train your body when it's time to wind down. Go to sleep at the same time every night. Wake up at the same time every morning and set an alarm. Create a set routine for it so your body has some sort of rhythm.

Ideas for nighttime rituals include practicing gratitude, writing a gratitude list about the day, praying, journaling, and doing five to ten minutes of yin yoga or a ten-minute guided meditation.

You can thank yourself and celebrate yourself for being alive and for doing the best you could. Find five things to be grateful for. Find five reasons to celebrate yourself today. It's whatever feels authentic to you.

No thinking in bed rule

If you are like me, when you go to bed your brain starts to go crazy with thoughts. If this happens to you, practice a no-thinking policy in bed. Your bed is a sanctuary. Treat your time there like meditation. When you're in bed, focus on your breath. When you go to sleep and catch yourself thinking, just come back to focusing on your breath.

Don't try to figure your life out in bed (or late at night). Don't think about your regrets or panic about the future. You're probably already exhausted and unable to think straight or clearly at 10 p.m. Come back to your breath, practice self-compassion, and let yourself figure it out tomorrow. Again, your bed is a safe place for sleep, not a place for your brain to punish you.

If you find yourself up late thinking in bed, it's helpful to get out of bed and go outside, take a bath, and ground.

You don't need to solve problems when you're trying

to go to sleep. You can just celebrate the day and all you got done. If you have to do something in bed, practice focusing on your breath and meditating or finding things to be grateful for.

Integrate:

Create a nighttime routine for you that feels good that includes reducing stimulation and wind-down practices.

2. If you find yourself thinking in bed, get up and do a practice that calms and soothes you.

Sleep

I mentioned this earlier, but sleep is so important for mental health. Prioritize it. Depression can affect your sleep in a big way, often compelling us to sleep more or less than we need. A lack of good nourishing sleep can wreck you.

Make sure you get enough sleep. Again, every body is different, so find what works for you. Most people need eight hours. Make an effort to fall asleep at the same time, and wake up at the same time, then go outside first thing when you wake up to reset your rhythm. This is so important.

Also, going to bed at 9 p.m. or 10 p.m. and waking up at 6 a.m. or 7 a.m. is a huge difference from going to sleep at

1 a.m. and waking up at 9 a.m. or 10 a.m. Experiment and find what works best for you. I know my life and routines play out in vastly different ways when I wake up at 6 a.m. compared to 9 a.m.

Preparing for Bad Days

One last valuable suggestion I have for self-care is to plan ahead for bad days. In my journal, I have a page of all the things that offer me relief when I'm having a hard day. This way, if and when I'm spiraling, I can just open to that page and see if any ideas on the list might help me.

When we're having a particularly hard day, it can be difficult to think clearly, and this planning ahead method can help.

When you are having a good day, take time to write out a list like this. What do you need the most when you're having a hard day? What reminders do you need to hear? What offers relief?

Integrate:

3. Get out your journal and write out a list of everything that soothes you when you're having a hard day. This is your new go-to list when you're having a hellish day.

Do the Best You Can

I know how hard it can be to take care of yourself when you're depressed.

I know you probably lack the energy, motivation, self-worth, and belief to do some or all of these things. So just do the best you can. Meet yourself where you are at, and celebrate every step. Make it fun. Start small to make big meaningful changes.

If you're learning to meditate, start with ten minutes a day. Don't start with an hour. Build up from there. If you miss a day, or a week, or a month, or a year and fall off, so what? Just start over. Or maybe meditation isn't for you. Try something else.

Celebrate your wins. Don't be mean to yourself for what you can't do. Focus on what you do instead of what you can't do. My big point is: don't beat yourself up or punish yourself.

I couldn't walk into a gym and bench five hundred pounds on my first try. I couldn't sit down for more than fifteen minutes to write when I started this book. It took me a year before I was able to sit for four-hour sessions to finish it. When you're trying to implement these ideas, do it with self-compassion.

I also want to note these areas separately are all huge overhauls in your life. Take time to explore, integrate, and change them. It can take a while to change your diet or find a routine for sleep or exercise that works for you. Take your time. The most important thing is that it has to work for you and serve you.

Chapter Five:

HOW TO TALK ABOUT
YOUR DEPRESSION
Conversations on Sasquatch

"So what's it like having a mental health problem?" she asked me point blank with the tone of a gossipy high school cheerleader chewing gum and twirling her hair.

I went slack-jawed. "Excuse me?"

It was the first question I was ever asked for my band's first interview.

We were a baby band and had only released four songs. I'd never spoken out about depression or my mental health to anyone before. She listened to my lyrics and made the leap that I was insane and had mental health problems.

I discovered that talking about mental health with other people would prove to be one of the wackiest and wildest journeys to parallel my actual mental health journey.

A year after that interview, I found myself sitting in my manager's office, looking above his desk at a massive portrait of a smirking Groucho Marx smoking a cigar, and waiting for him to get off the phone to start the meeting.

On paper, everything looked right. I was twenty-one, halfway through making my first album with my dream producer. My band was signed to an incredibly kind and supportive indie label that was paying for all of it. I'd gotten to the place that I'd always dreamed of, and I expected that I would feel amazing, or at least just a little better than I did.

My inner reality was the opposite. I was smack in the middle of my first major depressive episode, still living in the haunted house, and was so overwhelmed that I wanted life to just stop. Because no one ever explained to me what depression or anxiety attacks were, they were both undiagnosed and unexplained. I had no clue what was happening to me, but I knew I was in pain beyond belief and having the worst time ever.

I was hovering in the uncertainty of whether I should keep living, if this life thing was really worth it, while newly obligated by contract to finish the record I was in the middle of making.

My manager could tell something was wrong because we hadn't talked in a week or two. He called a meeting and wanted to know how the record was coming. He finally got off the phone and said, "In my forty-five years of being in the record industry, I've never seen an artist as miserable as you making their first record. Usually artists get to this point, and they are ecstatic, can't stop talking about it and are having the time of their lives making it . . . and you . . . well . . . what's wrong?"

I wasn't sure what was happening to me either or how to answer the question, so I mumbled, "I don't know. I think I'm depressed."

The energy in the room shifted to discomfort and then anger. His response was, "If you're so depressed, you might as well just go kill yourself."

It wasn't exactly the gentle emotional support I was looking for. I remember the shock of it felt like I was blacking out, and the room and my reality were melting. He was one of the first people I'd opened up to about my mental health, someone I looked up to for guidance, and this was his response. It shattered me.

If there ever was a confirmation of my unworthiness for being on the planet, it was this. Someone older, successful, and supposedly trustworthy was telling me to kill myself.

My overwhelming conclusion from this incident was that I would never open up to anyone about my mental health again or share how I genuinely felt with anyone. It didn't feel safe.

Why would I be vulnerable or talk to anyone about my depression when this is what happens? The pain of opening up to someone and having them attack me for it was so strong, I never wanted to feel it again.

After this fiasco, I went a whopping eight years without talking about depression. It was one of the dumbest decisions I ever made, but it made sense considering my experience.

It took me nearly physically breaking down and my entire life caving in before I was forced to admit to another person out loud that I was depressed.

Talking about mental health with other people can sometimes seem more like a conversation on aliens or Sasquatch; everyone has their own insane ideas and wildly different uninformed opinions and theories on it, based on God-knows-what they read on the internet. Depression is weird because, for whatever reason, there is still not a universal consensus that it is a real condition that will take a sledgehammer to your life.

If I told someone I had a broken bone, no one would suggest that I should just get my tarot cards read. If I told a friend I had diabetes, they wouldn't say, "Oh, think positive and it will clear up. Just read some Tony Robbins." Or imagine if I told a friend I had herpes and they said, "What do you have to be herpes about? There's nothing in your life to be herpes about."

Talking about depression is hard and scary. It's rolling the dice. You risk vulnerability to the point of self-oblivion. We don't know how people will react. How they react and how you make meaning out of their reaction can either save you or send you further down the hellhole.

This is why I wanted to devote a chapter to the importance of talking about your depression, how to talk about it, and how to consciously make meaning from and move through reactions in a healthy way.

Talking about Mental Health Is Mandatory

One of my favorite quotes on taking risks is from the movie Raging Bull. The trainer says to the boxer, "If you win, you win; if you lose, you win." This is how talking about mental health works. Talking about your depression is mandatory, and it is always a risk worth taking.

The positive benefits always outweigh the negative. The best-case scenario is it will save your life. The worst-case scenario is that you might be attacked or judged or feel isolated, like what happened with my manager. But here's why it's still worth it.

Reasons to Talk about Your Mental Health with Other People

You Actually Get Help

If no one knows you are hurting, no one can help you. Silence doesn't offer us the opportunity to heal like honest communication does. People can't read minds.

When I chose to be silent about my mental health, I became a really good liar. My silence cut off all authentic and genuine human connections in my relationships because I wasn't speaking or living my truth. I was always "fine." This silence and lying further isolated me from everyone in my life because no one got to see the real me.

Of course, no one recommended therapy or plant medicine or antidepressants to me because no one knew I was hurting that bad. You get back what you give and reflect. I gave off a coldness and "everything is fine" vibes and, in response, attracted people who could never see me or be there for me.

When I eventually did come out about my depression, a handful of people didn't believe me because they only saw the "rock star" and funny version of me. They never even got a glimpse of the real me.

Please, speak out about your mental health. Express it. Find someone you trust. Find a safe outlet, a container of allies you feel safe with, whatever that means to you, whether that's a therapist, close friends, family, or a support group. Really open up to them, and don't hold back. I know this can be terrifying, but if you take anything away from my book, please let it be this. Let someone know the pain you're in.

We Realize We Aren't Alone

We aren't meant to do life alone. We aren't meant to fight and solve all of our problems by ourselves. We can't. We need support from other people. We need their help, guidance, and wisdom, and one day the next generation will need ours. Healing yourself from mental health isn't a solo journey. You do not need to do this alone.

There is no honor in bearing unbearable emotional weight alone. The honor is being strong and courageous enough to say, "I am hurting. I am suffering. Can you please help me?" We need a community to talk about our problems with. The best athletes have coaches. You should have people in your corner, whether it is a therapist, a men's or women's group, a spiritual advisor, a shaman, or a life coach.

Talking helps us realize we are never alone in our pain and suffering. Talking about it helps us hold each other's hands in this journey called life. Other people who are healed and highly evolved have been in the exact same pain we are and have come out of it stronger and happier.

You Lose Your Separateness

Depression is all about separateness. It wants us to believe we are separate from life, from other people, from love. Separateness is suffering, and separateness is also an illusion. When we talk about our depression, we lose the illusion of separateness.

If you think about the history of humanity, you are not the first or last person to be depressed. You are also not the first or last person to believe their problems are beyond repair and that suicide is the only answer.

Your suffering is not special. It's not even new. Whatever problem you think you have, I guarantee you there are millions of people before you who've suffered through variations of it and millions after you who will suffer through it.

There is an inherent paradox that none of your emotions are unique to yourself, yet all of them are. Depression wants us to forget that we are part of the collective consciousness and that we are part of everyone and everything.

Because you are not the first or last person to feel how you feel, you are also not alone or unique in your suffering. There is a kinship here. Your sadness is not only yours, but everyone's. Someone else's sadness is your own. Your pain is the world's pain. There is nothing new under the sun, but we are together, interwoven in what we feel.

A side note and small gift is that depression, in this way, can be seen as a gift, a vehicle for empathy. When you hear of someone else suffering, you know what it's like, have compassion for them, and can be there for them.

Speaking Moves Energy

Speaking your truth is energy flow. Talking moves energy. It gets it out of your head, mind, and body and moves it into the air and ether. Talking creates space.

There is power in speaking aloud raw, radical honesty with good intentions. When you don't speak your truth, you cut off that flow. When that flow is cut off, the energy stagnates in your body and things become overwhelming. Better out than in.

Depression Loses Its Power

When we speak about our depression and anxiety, they begin to lose their power over us. Talking takes overwhelming abstractions that are swirling in your head and makes them manageable and identifiable. Our suffering becomes more tangible and less scary.

We might not be able to think of solutions for our suffering and be tortured by it, but someone else might be able to offer help in a direct and simple way.

It Helps Sort Out the People in Your Life

If you open up about your depression and are attacked, misunderstood, or judged for it, it's painful as hell but also a blessing in disguise.

You learn who understands your plight, who you feel safe with, and who might judge you for it. You learn where you can find safety and where you can't, and you start to let go of the people who don't need to be in your life. This clears room for those who are meant to be there.

Plus, when you start communicating authentically,

you'll start attracting people who see you for who you truly are and who will be able to love, help, and support you no matter what your emotional state is.

If someone else's response isn't what you wanted or expected, there is always an insight or lesson to be learned about yourself or other people in your life. It stings, but I'm going to help you figure out how to navigate that later in this chapter.

What Happens When We Don't Talk about It

The arguments for not talking about your mental health are probably more potent than the reasons to talk about it.

A One-Sided War

When I chose not to talk about my depression, it meant that there were no other voices or opposing viewpoints besides the toxic narratives in my head.

My entire life became a one-sided war with no dissent.

It was like a fascist regime had marched into the country of my head, and my response by remaining silent on my mental health was, "Come in, the beds are made, and I've readied the alcohol, prostitutes, and guns. Make yourselves at home."

Depression and anxiety ran wild and took over my thoughts, belief systems, daily actions, habits, self-talk, and narratives unchecked.

I lost all perspective on my life and "problems." All narratives got blown out of proportion, most times creating vastly alternative realities in my head. All of my "problems" grew to Godzilla-like sizes and became seemingly impossible to solve.

The joke here is that my problems and life situations weren't actually getting worse, my perception of them was. If I had someone to talk to, such as a therapist, I would have had help turning these seemingly imposing life-or-death situations into easily fixable scenarios.

Shame

When we don't speak about our mental health, shame takes over. We start to believe that, out of all the humans that have ever existed, our pain, suffering, and problems are so special, unique, unfixable, and one-of-a-kind that we are imaginably alone and our pain and hurt and our life are truly beyond redemption. Shame tells us we are bad, wrong, damaged, and unworthy.

Shame is a vicious cycle because it leads to more silence, which leads to more shame.

I think people kill themselves because they don't talk about their mental health, and the shame and hopelessness around their situation become unbearable. Depression tells them their problems are not solvable, and there's no way out, and that there's something irrevocably damaged about them.

With enough shame and silence, I became undoubtedly certain that my life was so beyond repair that there was no solution other than death.

To me, suicide eventually made sense because it was my brain's only answer to the great promise of relief; a breath of fresh air, getting a break from myself. My brain was incapable of thinking in any sort of positive way, and this was the only way my brain was telling me to get out of the pain. Of course, that was bullshit.

Now that we know speaking about mental health is mandatory and the dangers of staying silent, let's speak about who we should talk to. You can't just talk to anyone. You need tools to navigate the ridiculous reactions you might receive. Let's talk about that.

People Are Good

If you ask for help, most people generally and genuinely want to help you. Yet, so often with depression, people have no idea how to help you. In fact, what they think is help just makes a mess instead.

Everyone is doing the best they can with the tools and consciousness they have at the moment. Someone else's version of loving, helpful advice might sound like a "fuck you" to you.

Consider Who You Are Talking To and Why

You wouldn't ask a vegan about the best places to buy meat. Similarly, you wouldn't go to a dentist for a broken leg. So why would you ask anyone who doesn't know anything about depression for advice?

A lot of people have no vocabulary for mental health yet are still willing to give you loads of opinions and advice on it. It's wacky, I know. It would be like me giving advice to a football team about how to get the ball in the basket.

Be mindful of who you talk with about your mental health. I realized that when I started speaking out about mental health, it was a double-edged sword. It helped people and also brought on unwelcome responses.

People who have never experienced depression or anxiety should not tell you what to do about anxiety or depression.

Remember that whenever you ask someone for advice, or they just start giving it to you, it's coming from their own belief system, past, and life experience. Whatever they tell you is based on what they know. You have to strongly consider where they are coming from and what it is grounded in.

Here are some questions to ask before you open up about your mental health.

- Why are you talking to this person specifically? Could they offer a unique perspective?

- What are you expecting to get from the conversation? Are these expectations realistic based on whom you're speaking with?
- Where are they coming from? What is their background/belief system?
- How have they acted in the past when you've opened up to them?
- Does it feel safe for you to talk to them about this? Do you trust them?

One last thought: In addition to considering the who, please consider the when. Some of the biggest mistakes I've made have been times when I threw out a comment about my mental health in passing.

It's important to consider when to talk about mental health as well. Make sure you're in a moment when there is space for what you shared to be heard and the other person has the capacity to hear you.

How to Navigate the Reactions

When I got sober and started taking antidepressants, I pulled a one-eighty and went from not speaking about my mental health to only talking about it. I had nothing else to talk about.

The first night I went out sober, a drunk friend asked me how I was doing. I told him I had been suicidal, I had just started medication, and I was nervous as hell because I was the only one sober and didn't know what to do with my hands.

He leaned in and asked in a lowered voice, "Do you have any of those on you?" This guy was actually trying to buy and get wasted on ten milligrams of Lexapro.

When I started sharing my story, I quickly learned that ninety percent of people were supportive, receptive, kind, and open; and most of the time, sharing my story seemed to genuinely help people. There was a kinship in the suffering. "We're in this together." That made life worth it as far as I'm concerned. It was the best feeling in the world. I was helping people by being honest, and that made everything worth it.

The other ten percent was met with confusion or baffling bullshit. Here's how to deal with that.

Understand That It Has Nothing to Do With You

When it comes to talking about your own depression, more often than not, other people's reactions have absolutely nothing to do with you. It is usually entirely about the other person.

A lot of people don't know what to do with their own emotions, thoughts, and feelings, so when you share something you are struggling with, they often react to how your words make them feel instead of thinking in a clear and conscious way. When people react, they sometimes aren't really present with you or see you for who you actually are.

It becomes about them. They project their own fear and pain onto you.

Case in point, I've told family members about my depression and they began to search themselves for how they raised me wrong or where they messed up. They blamed themselves, saying, where did I go wrong? Which ironically makes it more about them than holding space for me. They missed the point entirely. I didn't feel seen, and they felt terrible.

Sometimes when you open up to someone, you trigger something in them—an emotion or event—that causes them to feel inner pain, and they react to the discomfort inside of themselves brought on by your words instead of you and your actual situation. It takes a lot of consciousness to presently respond to what someone else is saying instead of subconsciously being triggered. To really hold space for someone consciously without judgment so they feel seen and heard is a superpower.

Knowing where your expression ends and someone's projection begins is a huge step toward freedom in being able to talk about your mental health authentically without fear. It's a special kind of freedom when you are able to express yourself honestly and not care how other people take it. It is a practice that takes courage and awareness.

The only job you have is to speak your truth authentically and as honestly as you can. It's not your burden to care or worry about how other people take your truth. That being said, it's still really painful to not feel seen or understood by those we want to be seen and understood by.

Know that the most important thing is how you feel. Don't let anyone invalidate how you feel. No one else knows how you feel or can tell you how to feel.

How to Deal With Anger Reactions

If someone reacts with anger, it could be because they love you, feel afraid and helpless, or don't know how to best help you or be there for you. Anger is a mask for pain and fear. They are afraid because they feel so helpless, not knowing how to support you, and feel so terrible that you are suffering that they just blow up.

Anger says more about the person's inability to process their own feelings than anything about your own life situation. Anger or frustration says that a person is in pain and doesn't know what to do with it, so they pass it on to the next person.

Or maybe that person was in the same situation when they were young, and when they opened up to someone emotionally, they were met with anger, and they subconsciously learned that that's an appropriate way to react to others when they open up. Tough love. Now that's their behavior.

How to Deal With Shame Reactions

The one time I went to my Greek Orthodox Church in the past five years, my great uncle came storming up to me, saying, "I saw what you wrote on Facebook about being depressed."

He paused, looked me up and down, and said, "You live in Santa Barbara; you have a good family, a nice car, and a music career. What do you have to be depressed about? There's nothing in your life to be depressed about!"

To add to the shame he was serving me, he pulled the, "There are starving kids in *insert third world country*, and they would kill to have what you have."

Believe me, if anyone already hates who they are, hates how they feel, wishes they could pull themselves out of it and feel different, and feels deep shame about it, it's depressed people.

When I was lost in it, I could rationally understand how lucky I was to have the work, family, and living situation I had. But feeling it, knowing it, believing I was worthy of it, and accessing gratitude as a way of being was fucking impossible because I was in inescapable pain, terrified, and stuck in loops I couldn't break from. I then piled on shame, guilt, and disgust toward myself for not being able to feel how lucky and blessed I was.

People with depression don't feel blessed or lucky. People with depression feel screaming shame about being unable to access joy or gratitude.

When people respond with this, it's like they look at your external world and are baffled that there's a chance it doesn't match your inner emotional world. How can you live in a nice place and be depressed? How can you have money and be depressed?

People who say this usually think it's a choice to be depressed or have no idea what depression is because they've never experienced it.

It hurts because they are neglecting to see someone for who they are. It also discounts and shames someone for how they feel.

It's like they're saying your pain isn't real because they can't see it. They looked at the car you drive and it doesn't add up. Then added judgment is heaped on: You have a beautiful life, and you're pissing on it.

They are the emotion police, basically saying you're wrong for feeling how you feel (or, those feelings don't even exist in the first place), and instead of feeling that pain, you should be feeling this instead.

I've mainly gotten this response from older generations, which I think is due to a matter of consciousness as well as how they were raised and taught how or how not to emote. They have different values, different stigmas, and entirely different codes for mental health. Sometimes talking to them about mental health is as effective as looking to a priest to buy narcotics.

Similarly, there is still a segment of the population who

have never experienced depression and don't believe it's a real thing. A close friend of mine was like this.

But understand, just like I might never have to deal with over-sweating armpits or eating disorders, someone else will never understand or have to deal with depression.

Find a Therapist

If you only take one thing from this chapter, let it be this. Find a therapist. It's mandatory. When I was coming out of depression, my therapist saved my life. It's still, to this day, one of the most important decisions I've ever made.

If you have healthcare, they might have a list of therapists you can see for free or at an affordable rate. Sometimes universities offer free therapy.

Treat therapy like dating. Be willing to try a few people to see what styles you like. If something doesn't feel right, change it.

I'll never forget going to a therapist for the first time and telling him, "My band is signed, I just made my first record, I'm about to tour, and all I want to do is die." He looked at me, paused, and said with a bit of bitterness, "That had been my lifelong dream." I swore off therapy for years after that.

You should feel safe to be yourself. Find a therapist you can trust and who you don't feel judged by. Find one who sees you. They are there to help you.

I have a lot of friends who had an off-putting therapy experience and swore off the whole thing, which is unfortunate. It's kind of like going on a bad date and swearing off all romance.

It's also kind of insane how many friends of mine have therapists that they don't feel safe with or lie to. So find someone you feel safe being honest with. Find someone you love who fits with whatever kind of style you need.

Your Mental Health Journey Is a Superpower

Growing up, no one in my family, friend group, or school spoke about mental health. No one in my family ever talked about mental health, yet quite literally everyone in my family tree was affected by it. Depression, anxiety, mania, panic attacks, alcoholism, and suicide were as familiar to my Greek family as spinach is to spanakopita.

So, as a teenager, when I started having panic attacks, it never registered to me that something was wrong. I didn't even have a word for panic attacks or anxiety. I just knew I felt like I was exploding all the time. I naively thought, I guess this is who I am, and this is what happens. Because no one talked about it, I didn't think it was a problem or felt like I needed to talk about it.

It led me to have a "bend over" approach to all things mental health. It was just something you lived with, did nothing about, and hoped for the best. Depression and anxiety came at me with their suffering and I took it, no questions asked.

Because no one talked about it, and I didn't mention it to anyone, it never occurred to me that there was something I could do about it. So, I soldiered on, normalizing all of it. I just called it life.

For whatever reason, in certain cultures, mental health is still taboo. No one talks about it, but nearly everyone is affected by it at one point or another.

When we don't talk about it, we don't teach people what to do with these weird things called feelings and emotions. How can we teach people healthy coping mechanisms when we don't teach them about potential emotional hazards along the road?

It makes perfect sense people drink, do drugs, or kill themselves because they're doing the best they can with the unconscious coping mechanisms they were taught or had demonstrated to them as kids. Life becomes a fend-for-yourself game. You do whatever you can to cope.

When we don't talk about mental health to the next generation or give them a toolkit of healthy coping responses, it's like throwing them on a basketball court during a playoff game with a blindfold on, not knowing what team you're on or what position you are, or even the basic rules of basketball. Then someone hands you a ball and says, "Go win."

It's hard to win a game when no one explains the rules.

It's hard to express through language when no one has taught you the alphabet.

By talking about your own mental health, you can be the link and chain to affect the next generation. Speaking about your mental health can give others a voice and help them along their paths. Your mental health journey and voice can be a superpower for others on their path and can help them heal.

Ways to Integrate This Chapter

- Write down five people in your life you feel safe sharing your mental health journey with. This is your tribe.
- Write down five people in your life you don't feel safe sharing your mental health journey with.
- *Reflection & Reframe Journal Prompt:* Think about any horror stories you've had when talking about your mental health. Write on that experience, and reflect using the How To Navigate Reactions section to reframe the experience. How did they react? Was it even about you? Put yourself in the shoes of the other person; imagine where they are coming from and what they know. Write about the response you would have loved to hear from them and anything the current version of you needs now.
- Start taking steps to find a therapist you trust.

Chapter Six:

THOUGHTS

A Yoga Teacher Training Gone Horribly Wrong

The room was so hot it made a summer day in Iraq seem brisk. The collective sweat of twenty people dripped down the walls, and I was shocked I didn't see plumes of smoke as the sweat evaporated when it hit the ground. I've probably sweated out twenty pounds of my body weight in the past half hour alone. People around me were falling to their knees with a thud, nearly passing out. I couldn't tell if it was a war zone or a yoga class.

A drill sergeant masquerading as a power yoga teacher was barking orders along the lines of "Find your edge, then move past it and destroy it!" My entire body was shaking as I held a two-minute-long plank pose, thinking, I paid twenty-five hundred dollars for this? It was the fifth yoga class I'd taken that day, and I was in the middle of a nine-week yoga teacher training.

When I was in the denial phase of depression, I had a stroke of brilliance that maybe a yoga teacher training would fix me. I'd already tried to see if getting famous in a rock band would work, and it didn't, so I thought maybe this would work.

Other people were going into the yoga training with a desire to get a better butt, do handstands for Instagram, or actually become yoga teachers. I had no desire to be a yoga teacher. I was just looking to stop my suffering and find some kind of goddamn relief from the existential despair I was in.

What I was expecting to get out of this training was sort of like walking into Mcdonald's expecting a five-course meal and a Thai massage. The women running the training were about as equipped to deal with a suicidal musician looking to fix deep wounds as a four-year-old with a plastic kitchen being ready for a job interview at a Michelin star restaurant.

As I was holding the plank, trying not to black out from the heat, a thought came to me. It was almost like someone whispering in my ear. The voice wasn't angry or mean. It was simple. It said, "Kill yourself."

I looked around the room, confused. Did anyone else hear that? I tried to come back to my breath and keep in the flow. But in the span of the day, it kept coming again and again.

At that time, my relationship with my own thoughts was pretty simple. I believed everything I thought. A thought came in, and I took it as the capital T truth. If it's a thought, and it's in my head, it must be true. If it's telling me I should kill myself, I guess I should kill myself. I'd completed a lot of school, but no one had ever told me what to do with my thoughts.

As this twelve-hour day wore on, and the instructors were telling us how to properly pronounce savasana and what to do with pregnant women in class, I was having my own inner storm. The thought would not go away. It kept pounding against my brain: kill yourself, kill yourself, kill yourself. Confusion turned into horror and panic.

That day ended, but the thought didn't. The day became weeks, months, and eventually years of this thought wreaking havoc.

It felt like it was everywhere. It came between chaturangas; before, during, and after I had sex. It was in every part of the writing and recording of my songs. It came at dinner with friends, where I would escape to the bathroom to splash water on my face and give myself a stay-on-this-planet pep talk, trying to compose myself enough to feign sufficient presence and interest to hear a friend droll on about their bathroom renovations. It was often the first thought as I woke up and the last when I went to sleep.

The more I tried to run from the thought, the louder it

became. The more I tried to fight it, the bigger and uglier it got. It grew into a force. I was terrified to be left alone with my mind.

I feared the thought. I feared anything that came out of my head. I feared my brain, which was seemingly hellbent on self-annihilation 24/7. I didn't know what to do with it or any of the thoughts exploding in my head.

In addition to this thought, I continued to pile resistance, shame, fear, guilt, anger, and self-hatred onto that thought. I added a seven-layer shit cake on top of it. It became a daily alchemy that turned that single raindrop of a thought into a full-blown category five hurricane (more on this idea to follow).

What's wrong with me that I think this? I wish it would stop. I kept thinking.

If I had known what I know now, I would have realized it was just a thought. It's not who I am. But at the time it felt like a devastating force wrecking my life. That thought and my reaction managed to uplevel my already brutal depression and send me off the rails. This is why I'm dedicating a chapter to thoughts.

This chapter is about your thoughts: what to do with them, how to move through them consciously, and how they relate to depression. The quality of the relationship we have with our thoughts equals the quality of life we have.

The relationship we have with our own thoughts can make us a billionaire or send us to an asylum. They can destroy us or make all our dreams come true.

There is the classic saying, "The mind is a terrible master, but a great servant." I often think of David Foster Wallace's This Is Water, where he says, "It is not the least bit coincidental that adults who commit suicide with firearms almost always shoot themselves in the head. They shoot the terrible master."

Depression and anxiety tend to be monsters of the mind. Depression speaks to us in thoughts. These thoughts are often pulverizing and originate from the Greatest Hits mindsets from Chapter 3, like fear, self-doubt, self-hate, envy, anxiety, pessimism, lack, limit, and victimization.

I bet no one has asked you, what is the relationship you have with your thoughts? Do you believe them? Do you run from them? Are you afraid of them? Are you a prisoner to them, caged in, terrified, and alone? Do you realize you have a choice and power in what and how you think? Or do you consciously move through them and make an effort to change how you think? Having a better relationship with your thoughts will help you navigate your depression. Here are a couple thoughts on thoughts.

Thoughts on Thoughts

You Are Not Your Thoughts

You are not your thoughts. You are consciousness witnessing the thoughts. If thoughts are clouds, you are the sky. In the same way that clouds are not the sky, you are not your thoughts. Clouds are changing and moving all the time, and so are your thoughts. You are the witness, the unmoving boundless consciousness of sky behind it all.

Just Because You Think Something, Doesn't Mean It's True

In my yoga nightmare, I was missing one of the biggest holy shit realizations about thoughts. Just because we think something doesn't mean it's true. Just because a thought comes into our head, telling us something about ourselves, doesn't mean it's valid or real. Thoughts are wild, wacky, and bizarre. Most of them move fast and don't want us to notice them.

This is something to be vigilantly mindful of when talking about depression because the quickest way to buy ourselves a first-class ticket to suffer-town is to believe all we think and take all our thoughts as truth.

Depression screams thoughts like, "I don't deserve to be alive," "I'm unworthy of life," "My life is fucked," etc. Depression is a liar and a storyteller. Not all we think is true.

One caveat. Although you aren't your thoughts, you are what you think about. Buddha said, "What you think about, you become." This is how our thoughts can create carnage.

Thoughts = Beliefs = Actions

Most times, behind every thought is a belief. We then make decisions and take action based on those beliefs. Beliefs create thoughts, and thoughts create habits, which manifest into actions and decisions. This is why it's so important to watch what we think and notice our reactions to our own thoughts.

A thought like, "Kill yourself" or "I'm a failure" could stem from a belief of unworthiness like, "I don't believe I deserve to be alive." Then you begin to act and make decisions from that place. For example, you may think, "I won't take the risk and ask her out because I'll never be good enough for her," or "I'll never get that job because I don't deserve to be alive and therefore don't deserve anything good in my life." You don't have the self-esteem or belief in possibility because you think your life is a mistake.

What's especially vicious is then we make decisions from a place of unworthiness, fear, lack, and survival. We attract unfortunate people and situations into our life that confirm our unworthiness. This can make our depression worse and affirm our unworthiness and shame.

You don't believe you're worthy of a good partner or job, so you attract a low-energy job that's entirely unfulfilling or settle for an abusive partner. These situations affirm to us our unworthiness and are most times unhealthy, unkind, or unfulfilling.

Now you have external proof. If my boss and girlfriend think I'm the bane of the earth, I must be. I don't deserve to be alive. This just leads to more despair, powerlessness, depression, and hopelessness in your life and situations, and the cycle repeats.

Our thoughts are creating our realities all of the time. This is why it's so important to watch what we think, and also why I asked you in Chapter 2 to notice what comes up for you as you read this book.

A Thought Alone Is Nothing

A thought by itself holds no weight. It's the emotions, narratives, energy, beliefs, and reactions we give it that send us to heaven or hell. In other words, a thought is just a thought. By itself, it's like a balloon with no air.

Two people could have the same exact thought, and it could terrify one person but not faze the other. The difference is everything behind the thought and how we unconsciously or consciously react to it. It's when we unconsciously begin to color the thought with emotional weight that we become triggered and lose our presence.

Our Responses to Thoughts Is Where Freedom Lies

How we react to our thoughts is the difference between freedom and prison.

A thought without a story is nothing. A thought with a story can end your life. What we feed, grows. There's a saying: "Energy flows where consciousness goes."

When I started seeing my therapist, I told her about the "kill yourself" thought. She suggested, "What would happen if you didn't run but just acknowledged it and sat with it? You're giving it power when you run from it."

I began to practice mindfulness and simply noticed when it came. I began to consciously choose to greet it like an old friend. Oh, welcome back. Good morning. I see you are here again for whatever reason.

As soon as I did this, the power dynamic shifted. It lost its power. Its voice softened. Its bite lost its teeth. As soon as I stopped giving it power, it lost its power over me.

The thought still came, and sometimes it still does, but now I greet it as a messenger and ally.

When it does come, I stop and pause to do inventory. Am I living in alignment? Is there something I need to change? What do you have to tell me? Is there a message here or a way I can take better care of myself? Is there something, an emotion or feeling, that I'm not willing to face? What am I ignoring that needs tending to?

The "kill yourself" thought went from terrorist to teacher. It took a lot of pain, suffering, and work to get to that place, but it was worth it.

Sacred Club Bouncers

To make this a bit more fun, I like to imagine that we are sacred club bouncers. Our lives and ways of being are the sacred club, and our thoughts are wily kids trying to sneak in and rage.

Using awareness and mindfulness makes the difference in who gets in and who doesn't.

Imagine what a nightmare it would be if you let everyone in without checking who and what they are and where they came from.

When you let everything in and believe everything without presence, when you take enough tickets or excuses for thoughts like, "I'm not good enough," soon there isn't room for thoughts like, "I'm worthy."

When we believe everything we think without question, this is what happens. Our beliefs, habits, and perceptions of life get chosen for us. This is what it means to live unconsciously. If we are not conscious about what we think, then unconscious thoughts run our lives. When it comes to depression, this can be a game changer. I'm hinting at a bigger picture here. There are two kinds of thinking: conscious and unconscious.

Unconscious Thinking

If we aren't vigilantly aware of what and how we think and how we react to thoughts, we run the risk of letting unconscious thoughts and patterns run our lives. This is terrifying and akin to being asleep at the wheel in our own lives. We risk falling into patterns and habits we aren't consciously aware of, controlled by beliefs, emotions, and thoughts we are not aware of. It's unconscious living at its finest, like being strapped in a rollercoaster blindfolded.

Conscious Thinking

On the other hand, if we can think unconsciously, we can also learn and choose to think consciously. Thinking consciously means we can choose what to think and how to think. We get to consciously decide how to make meaning out of what we think and, in turn, get to consciously choose our response.

With presence and mindfulness, we can slow everything down, watch our own thoughts as they emerge, examine them, and check their authenticity, truth, and how they serve us. Then, we get to decide if we want to rewrite those thoughts. This may sound simple, but when you consider that the quality of your thoughts equals the quality of your life, it's a super Saiyan power move.

This simple perspective shift means you are in charge of your thoughts; they are not in charge of you. You decide the weight and meaning to give what you think. Remember, we have the freedom and the power to make conscious meaning out of anything that happens to us in life, and thoughts are no exception.

Not only do we not have to believe what we think, but with consciousness, we can begin to have discretion about how and what we think and ultimately change our own story. What kind of thoughts do we want to let into the venues of our hearts and consciousness? We have the freedom to decide how to react to what we think.

Now that we have given some thought to thoughts, I want to talk about what to do when icky ones come up.

Watch Your Thoughts

To have a better relationship with yourself and your depression, simply begin to notice your thoughts.

There is a big reason the mindfulness chapter comes after this one. All of the concepts of mindfulness in the chapter can and should be applied to watching your thoughts. Watch them without judgment or narratives. Just begin to notice how and when they come up.

Your thoughts come out in conversations, actions, habits, writing, and obviously thinking. I want you to watch your thoughts because they are a brilliant insight into our underlying belief systems. Meditation and yoga are great tools of support to begin to watch our own thoughts.

Integrate: Thought Alchemy Practice

Depression and anxiety can cause us to think uncomfortable and scary thoughts.

Here is how I alchemize negative thoughts into thoughts that serve me. Anytime you are confronted with a thought that feels icky or uncomfortable, you can pause and ask these questions, practicing what I call "thought alchemy."

1. When a mean thought comes in, simply get curious. Pause, take a deep breath, and slow things down.

2. Write out or say out loud the thought that is uncomfortable for you.

3. First, welcome the thought. Give it a warm hello, a big yes. Allow and accept it. You can even thank it for coming. Don't resist any of it.

4. Notice and gently examine the thought:

Where do I feel this thought in my body?

What's the tone and voice of this thought?

What emotion is behind this thought?

What am I unwilling to feel?

What am I resisting?

What led me to this thought? (i.e., what was I doing or thinking right before this thought?)

What is the belief behind this thought?

Is this thought true? (Would my closest friend say this about me or agree with what it says?)

Is this thought something I would say to a close friend or loved one?

What do I stand to gain by believing this thought?

(Where does my life go, and where does this thought lead me if I believe this? For example, say the thought is, "I'm not good enough." It can lead you to turn down a job or romantic opportunity because you don't feel worthy.)

5. Alchemize the thought.

Now that we have this info, here is where we can transform the thought.

What thought could I replace this one with that would better serve me?

AKA: What is the opposite of this thought? How could I turn this into an affirmation? (For example, "I'm fat," becomes "I'm perfect as I am, and I love my body.")

What does this thought have to teach me?

What is the lesson here?

6. Lastly, thank this thought for coming into your life with whatever its message was, and thank it for being a teacher. If you don't need it, say "Thank you, I'm not in need of your services."

I've found it's really helpful to journal on this. When I was dealing with the "kill yourself" thought, I kept a bullet journal page of every time it came up and notated where I was, what I was doing right before it came up, and a positive thought to replace it with, like, "There is a purpose for my life."

This gave me empirical data. "Oh, I've had the 'kill yourself' thought in bed in the morning five times this week. Maybe I need to get out of bed." Or, "This thought flares up when I'm around this person. Maybe I need to spend less time with them." When we alchemize our thoughts, we can start to adjust our lives to better help and serve ourselves.

Every Thought Is a Teacher

We can see thoughts as teachers. They clue us into our belief system. They tell us where we need work and how we can better take care of ourselves. When we watch our thoughts, they can show us where we are stuck, reveal our self-limiting beliefs, and teach us how we can better take care of ourselves when we're suffering from depression.

When we pause to watch our thoughts, we can rewrite the stories.

The biggest beauty in this work is that you start to change the relationship you have with your thoughts. They are no longer terrorists but teachers because every thought is a chance to learn more about who you are, what you need, and how you can better take care of yourself. Instead of hurting you, thoughts will guide you.

Set Clear Intentions

Before every plant medicine ceremony, we go around in a circle and everyone shares their intention out loud. I've heard it all. Someone wants money, someone else wants to be at one with the universe, someone else wants to soften up and love themselves more.

I always feel a ping of nervous excitement because I don't want to get it wrong.

During one ceremony, people were having a particularly hard time coming up with clear intentions, so the shaman led us through this meditation I'm about to walk you through.

Something no one ever told me is that there are different areas of intelligence and guidance we can tune into. It's so Western to believe the head is the end-all-be-all master. We have the gift of tuning into our heart, our gut, our spirit, and our head. Our head provides only one piece of a larger dialogue we can attune to. Your body's intelligence is ancient.

This exercise is a brilliant way of learning how to listen to different parts of yourself. It's called the head, heart, and gut meditation. Simply put, you ask the same question to three different parts of your body and then listen for guidance.

Whenever you have a question about something, need to make a decision, want to set an intention or prayer, or don't know the next step, you can practice this.

Integrate: Head, Heart, Gut Meditation

1. Find a comfortable position, preferably sitting down, and take a few deep breaths. Relax your body, noticing and releasing any tension.

2. Formulate your question in the simplest way. Say you want to set your intention for the day. The question is, "What is my intention for the day?"

3. Ask your head, "What is my intention for the day?" Focus your awareness on where your head is. Then listen for answers. You'll know when it's done.

4. Ask your heart the same question, "What is my intention for the day?" Focus your awareness on your heart space. Again, listen for answers and notice what comes up.

5. Now, bring your awareness to your gut. Ask your gut the same question, "What is my intention for the day?" Repeat the same steps as above.

6. Lastly, thank your body for sharing its wisdom with you.

What's remarkable about this practice for me is that I usually have three radically different answers to the same question. My head is typically the slave driver and dictator who wants me to do and achieve. My heart is usually begging for presence, space, and being. And my gut offers deep spiritual and soul wisdom.

This practice gives you insight into different areas of your being. You start to recognize the patterns in your thoughts. I was able to trace back my desire to be productive all the time to a belief that my worth was tied to my productivity. We are just following the trails of where our thoughts lead.

Sometimes it takes practice to tune into different areas, especially if we've neglected them for a while. The first time I asked my heart for guidance, its response was, "Oh, now you want my wisdom?" It was a joke but also sad because I ignored it for a decade.

Depression can have us living in our heads, so this is why the head, heart, and gut exercise can be so helpful.

Try this when you feel depressed. This meditation can be a huge gift to help you know how to take care of yourself better. I've done this exercise multiple times a day whenever I have a question, and it never lets me down.

Most importantly, after you get the wisdom from your heart or gut, make sure to act on it.

Ways to Integrate This Chapter

- Keep a thought journal: Every time you have a thought that doesn't serve you, write it down and add it to the journal.
- Practice thought alchemy.
- Practice the Head, Heart, Gut Meditation whenever you are looking for guidance.
- *Journal Prompt:* Write about the relationship you have with your own thoughts. Get honest. Do you like how you think? What would you change? What is a way of thinking you'd like to step into?

Chapter Seven:
PRESENCE
Just Eat the Mushrooms, Babe

Forty-eight hours before I was face-first in a bush crying about reality, I was sitting in a circle with eight of my closest friends, listening to the shaman talk about what to expect before drinking Ayahuasca. It was the same sort of "keep your hands and legs in the vehicle at all times" talk that a Disneyland employee gives before the ride starts. Instead of what to do if the grandmother sitting next to you vomits on the Jungle Cruise, we learned what to do if we found ourselves in a potentially terrifying situation on Herculean-strong psychedelics quite literally beyond any reality our moms could have prepared us for.

I was expecting to hear some heroic advice about what to do if we encounter a demon beast on some hell plane in another dimension, but instead he gave us a single syllable acronym: S.A.L.

He said it stands for Surrender, Accept, and Let Go. "Resistance creates suffering," he said, and in ceremony, "if we fight what is happening to us, it just makes everything worse." He instructed us that whatever comes up on medicine, no matter how terrifying or scary, we should just surrender to it, accept it, and then let it go.

He also instructed that if and when we found ourselves stuck and struggling in a harrowing, otherworldly scene with the medicine, to ask, "What am I resisting?"

Naming our resistance brings it out of the shadows and into the light. By identifying it, we are able to cultivate presence and relax into what we are feeling, so we can respond in a conscious way. It's brilliant and simple advice and can be applied to every single aspect of our lives.

I recently got my ass handed to me by S.A.L. I learned what happens when you resist and refuse to accept the present moment.

I came home one day to my beaming girlfriend, who said, "Let's take mushrooms right now and go on a hike," as she pulled out two small brown chocolate boxes with golden hearts on the side.

It seemed like the worst idea of all time, and I had a laundry list of reasons why. It went against all of my scripts for taking medicine.

It was psychedelic Russian roulette. I had no idea how much of a dose we were taking. The bite-sized chocolate could be a mellow, giggle a lot kind of night, or nine hours of eternal terror, falling face-first into the void.

It was also 5:30 p.m., and I usually go to terrifying places when I take mushrooms at night, having had up-all-night panic attacks on mushrooms before.

We also had no plan or container, which to me was essential for medicine journeys. The plan was to go on a hike and see what happened and figure out how to get home somehow, praying that one of us still had cognizance of what arms were to drive home or to have the awareness to even grasp the very concepts of "car," "home," and "road."

I also like to have some sort of chance to mentally prepare and ground myself before medicine, which didn't seem to be an option as I looked up at my girlfriend grinning ear to ear saying, "Are you ready?"

I realized it was now or never, and something in my gut said "fuck it." We set intentions and ate the medicine.

Mushrooms can take anywhere from ten minutes to over an hour to kick in, and as we were looking for a parking space after the fifteen-minute drive to the Hollywood hike, I felt my arms start to dissolve and my torso burst with the energy of Source and all divine creation and thought. Oh fuck, oh fuck, oh fuck, this is a big dose, and it's hitting hard quick.

Despite having two years' worth of psychedelic experiences, I began to act like a psychedelic virgin. I forgot all my spiritual training and began to make every mistake in the book. I panicked.

When we got out of the car, I lost all concept of where my body ended and the air around it began. As we hiked, I started to freak out when the mountains and trees around me started to swirl and coalesce into one unified pattern, and I realized I was about to fully enter deep medicine space. I fought it like an ant fighting an oncoming tsunami.

The only thing my panicked brain could think of was to sprint. Maybe, I thought, if I sprint up this trail, the medicine won't hit as hard. What I didn't know was heavy breath work like, say, sprinting, activates the medicine and makes it hit quicker and harder.

I ran up the trail, got to the overlook, panting, and the medicine hit me like a truck. In an instant, the hike, the mountains, and the world blacked out, and I was in full medicine space, having a full-blown Ayahuasca-like experience.

When I came to, I found myself sitting on the ground, grasping my legs, rocking back and forth, having a meltdown, terrified and traumatized. The medicine had seen my resistance and reached me the only way it could; it forced me down, almost violently, and knocked me on my ass.

When I was able to stand up again, I was pissed. I entered full-blown resistance for the next three hours.

I was livid about being stuck on this mountain on medicine, having no idea how long it would last or when or how it would end, feeling completely helpless and out of control.

Why is this happening to me right now? I hate this. Did I really need this right now? This is not how I wanted this night to go. All I wanted was a goddamn vegan pizza and to cuddle, and now here I am on a pitch black trail, having a full-blown medicine journey that's awful, looking over a terrifying digital-looking L.A. skyline.

I stacked on shame and judgment. Why couldn't I have handled this better? I thought I was more woke than this. Don't I know better than to fight and resist?

I got so lost in the whirlwind nightmare of my own head with all of its fear-mongering, resistance, and spiraling out that I forgot entirely about my girlfriend.

When I had the presence of mind, I found her a few feet away from me. I wobbled over to check in and asked, "Babe, how are you? Are you ok?"

She was sitting cross-legged on the ground, practically buzzing. Grinning, lotus position, hands open to the sky, she looked up at me and said, "Yes, I'm talking to God. I'll see you in a bit."

I stood open-mouthed and stunned. Here we had two different people, eating the same medicine, with two different mindsets and tactics and two totally different results.

She was having one of the best nights of her life, in bliss town, talking to God, moving through deeply profound revelations and experiences, while I was stuck in hell, feeling alone, traumatized, and terrified.

She was in full acceptance of what was happening, and her journey was wonder and awe, while I went into full-blown resistance and jumped aboard the terror train. If only I had remembered S.A.L.

One of the main themes of this book has been about acceptance and resistance. We spoke about the bigger themes of accepting our depression, and now I want to speak on the daily, even moment-to-moment acceptance and resistance of our moods, emotions, and feelings.

We live our lives one moment at a time. Life is just one big present moment. Every time we look, we are in the present moment. Oh, look, we are always here, right now, again. We are nowhere else besides now.

All of our hope, hell, joy, depression, fear, love, and humanity is right here in the present moment. This eternal present moment is where all things are born. And that present moment is shifting, changing, and morphing all the time. Future and past exist only as concepts and illusions of the mind. We don't need to worry about the future because we never know how it will be when we get there, and we can't change anything about the past. The only power and freedom we really have is in the here and now; this very moment.

In the present moment, we always have two options: resistance or acceptance.

We either say yes to what is happening here and now, or we resist and fight it. We either S.A.L. or we fight. This goes for everything: thoughts, emotions, feelings, or taking your aunt Becky to get her colonoscopy. The story I told you about mushrooms is a great example of what happens when we resist the present moment.

Presence is key to finding relief for depression. Mindfulness is the practice that helps us reconnect with the present moment. Our relationship with mindfulness and the present moment determines the amount we suffer. Learning to say yes to the present moment offers us a safe haven and freedom from depression and anxiety. When we lose presence, depression runs wild, we start to believe its narratives, and we suffer. This chapter speaks of the importance of presence and mindfulness as a tool for navigating and healing when it comes to depression.

Two Worlds

I've mentioned having panic attacks a lot in this book. I wouldn't wish them upon anyone. They were physically and emotionally devastating. It felt like I was locked in the overhead compartment of an airplane and the plane was on fire crashing and spiraling down.

One night while having an attack, I walked through my kitchen and looked at a toaster and had a moment of clarity: This toaster is still a toaster. The toaster isn't on fire or freaking out about my life. My internal world was a universe apart from what was happening in the external world.

I realized that in every moment, there are two worlds: one in our head, and one that is actually here. At that moment, as I passed by the toaster, my head was in the apocalypse, screaming, "My life is over, I've fucked up beyond repair," and meanwhile, the toaster was just sitting there, being a toaster, calm, having no problem at all.

It was a lesson and testament to how powerful our thoughts and emotions are. My mind created all of this. I was worked up into a storm, but in reality, I was just in the kitchen at my parents' house. There was no immediate threat of danger, yet my body was screaming death, panic, and suffering.

It can be profound when we realize that most of the suffering of depression and anxiety is our minds creating the illusion of danger, telling us that we are not ok, not safe. This is the sort of wild illusionary and trance-like quality of depression and anxiety. They are both not real, and yet when we are getting annihilated by them, they seem stunningly real.

Presence and mindfulness come into the picture because they help us tell the difference between these two worlds.

Resistance

In life, when we fight and resist what is happening to us right here and right now, we suffer.

When we want things to be different from how they are in the present moment, we suffer.

When we want people to be different than who they are and don't accept them as they are, we suffer.

When we don't like how we feel and want to feel different and resist it, we suffer.

When we don't like how our lives are in the present moment and color it with narrative and resistance, we suffer.

When we resist our thoughts, we suffer.

When we don't like how depression makes us feel and we fight and resist it, we suffer.

All of our resistance comes from rejecting the present moment because reality isn't how we think it should be. We have an opinion on how our lives should be and how we think we should be feeling, and that rubs up against our actual experience of the here and now. Resistance is like a delusion. We can't clearly see things for how they are. Our heads and thoughts fight our bodies and spirits.

Often what's behind all this resisting is anger and fear. Fear that we will not be ok. Fear that we are not safe. Fear that we are alone or will be abandoned. And so on. Fear can lead to anger over feeling helpless that we lack control over situations, people, and outcomes. Anger arises in wishing we could change people or situations that we can't.

This fear and anger can lead us to check out, run, or self-abandon because it seems too painful to sit with the truth of our situation.

Depression and anxiety take over our lives when we resist the present moment. We become caught in their narratives like a fish taking bait.

Seven-Layer Shit Cake

To demonstrate what happens when we resist the present moment, I have a concept I call the Seven-Layer Shit Cake, which I introduced briefly before. Let's look a bit further.

It's when you feel and resist a single thought or emotion and begin to stack onto it other low-vibe and resistance-type feelings or narratives, like anger, shame, judgment, self-abuse, or frustration.

It's essentially the concept of taking a single raindrop and turning it into a Category 5 hurricane. Before you know it, you're dealing with a full-blown and unmanageable emotional hurricane of panic, judgment, and fear. I'll explain with an example.

Say you wake up and feel sad. This is the initial emotion. Getting out of bed seems impossible. Brushing your teeth or doing anything at all is like writing a PhD dissertation on metaphysics.

Your first reaction is, "Fuck. Another day I feel terrible. I hate that I feel like this."

Resistance.

Then you add judgment and narratives and mean thoughts. "What's wrong with me that I'm like this?"

Mix in some panic and hopelessness. "Will I ever get over this?"

Top it off with some dramatic absolutes and hopeless ultimatums. "I guess I might as well kill myself because I'll never get better."

This is a Seven-Layer Shit Cake. Now that initial sadness has become a full blown hurricane of negativity about your life. This is exactly what I did on mushrooms on the hike. I was in full-blown resistance mode, stacking on other stories and punishing myself for all of it.

The Seven-Layer Shit Cake takes the initial emotion and compounds it with more negative emotions. Instead of having to deal with that initial feeling of sadness, your mind has created a brutal imaginary universe where hopelessness, fear, and panic rule. This is how anxiety attacks are born and how depression gets all of its power.

We then ironically have to spend more time and energy working ourselves down from this ledge we've created.

What's worse is that this resistance is a closed loop. All resistance leads to more resistance. We send this energy out into the world, and this is what we attract. You become what you think about. If all day long you're thinking about how terrible everything is, odds are everything you see will be terrible, and you will attract terrible things into your life. Our thoughts create our reality.

All the time spent resisting is time spent killing the present moment and, in a sense, guaranteeing things won't get better or change. We could be using that same time and energy to dance with what is and actually bring about healthy change.

Acceptance

The other option in the present moment is full and radical acceptance. It's welcoming and saying yes to every emotion and thought as it comes up without fight, judgment, or narratives.

In every moment, we have the choice to say yes. Yes to whatever is here, no matter how icky, horrifying, or wild. There is no fight to saying yes; there is only flow and acceptance.

Taking that same example, you wake up feeling sad, and you say yes to it.

You wake up feeling sad. You accept it.

You decide to be with it. To breathe and lean into it. To feel it in all of its brutal splendor.

You notice the sensation of it in your body. You notice the unhelpful thoughts and narratives that come up and keep returning to your breath and the sensations.

You have space now to choose the voice of compassion. Tune in and ask yourself, "What do I really need here? Sadness, what are you trying to tell me?" Listen from a place of deep knowing instead of panic. Treat yourself like a precious jewel.

Even if you've had a hundred days of waking up in this same sadness, you can meet yourself where you are and accept it.

When we say yes, we tend to soften and flow. We see

everything as an opportunity, lesson, or gift. It's cocreating with life rather than getting beaten down by it.

Acceptance is a totally different path and leads to completely different results than resistance. The difference in our ability to choose acceptance or resistance lies in our ability to be present, awake, and conscious.

When we accept what is happening to us right here and now, we come into presence, which is where all our freedom and power are found.

What Is Presence?

Presence is the ability to exist consciously in this very moment. It's to be here and now with whatever is, well, here. It's simply watching what is happening now and noticing whatever is here without narratives or judgment. Presence is a practice of seeing what actually is; what's real versus what isn't. Its cost of entry is a single breath. Anyone and everyone can do it.

Presence is not always comfortable. It can be terrifying to be present with emotions like fear or sadness. But the way to process these emotions is by feeling them, accepting them, and allowing them to move through you. This point is so important. Having the courage to be present and feel everything is the path to healing.

Mindfulness is a practice that uses different focus techniques to return to the present moment. Mindfulness helps us to be present. Again, the whole point is to just practice watching and noticing thoughts, emotions, sensations, and feelings as they come up and not label, judge, or react to them. And if we do get lost in judgment or story, we notice that too and come back to the present moment (without adding a story on top of that), over and over again.

The gift of presence and mindfulness is that they give us the ability to notice what is happening in our minds, hearts, and bodies in real time, which then helps us get to know ourselves on a deeply intimate basis and helps us be better self guardians.

Presence and mindfulness offer us power, safety, and freedom from depression.

Stimulus and Response

Life is full of stimuli and responses. There is a stimulus, meaning something happens: a person punches us, a thought comes up, or we feel something. Then there is inevitably a response: we yell back, panic, blindly reach for a coping mechanism, or react with other thoughts or emotions.

The power of presence comes in noticing all of this. Presence helps us notice how we react to things, where we get caught, when we get angry, when we are happy, and when depression is peaking. The biggest superpower of presence is that it creates space between stimulus and reaction. This sacred space is where all of our freedom lies.

Presence offers us freedom because it slows things down to where we can consciously choose our own response to it. We feel an emotion like fear, but instead of reacting and panicking, we sit with it, curiously notice it, and experience it in its fullness.

We have sovereignty and choice now. When we start to notice the storms we create, we can begin to calm them. We don't get as caught in our own stories or the vicious pull of our emotions and feelings.

Negative thoughts still might come in, but we don't take their bait as much. We just notice them, then let them go and come back to our breath or whatever else anchors us in the present. Then we can tune into, listen, and know what we actually need and we can begin to take better care of ourselves. Here's an example of how presence, or lack of presence, works and the sacred space between stimulus and response.

I have this friend who is tall, handsome, and so effortlessly cool it's almost infuriating. I don't understand it. All his clothes fit perfectly, and he has a James Bond style. He exudes a rock star nonchalantness. Every time I'm around him, I feel like a frumpy and anxious Hobbit in drag.

One day we got lunch, and I was wearing a pair of sparkling bedazzled loafers I was really proud of. An older man walked up to me, paused, and deadpanned me in that way old men do when they have to search their ancient brains to remember how language works. He pointed down at my feet and, to my horror, snarled, "I don't like your shoes."

Without pause, I looked down at his shoes (atrocious brown dress shoes from Ross) and said, "Well, I don't like your shoes either."

He walked away, and I was left baffled and ashamed in front of my cool friend.

If I had access to more presence in that moment, I could have paused and explored different conscious reactions like compassion or mediation. Maybe he had shoe trauma or a foot fetish, and this was his childish way of hitting on me. If I stopped, maybe I could have empathized. How sad must his life be if he had to insult strangers? I felt compassion for anyone in his orbit. Instead, I unconsciously reacted and met his low vibes with my own low vibes.

Presence helps us widen the gap between stimulus and response so we can begin to consciously choose our reactions. This moment of pause between stimulus and response is a sacred space where we have all the freedom in the world.

Without presence, we aren't aware of our own thoughts, we aren't aware of our feelings, our emotions, our patterns, and we get taken hostage by whatever sensation comes our way. We have no equanimity. It's like being blindfolded on a rollercoaster of our own suffering.

Power, Safety, and Presence

To tie all of this together with depression, the safest place for any of us to be, especially those of us with depression, is in the present moment. When we lose presence, it feels like we lose our safety, power, and sovereignty.

The wrath of depression and anxiety takes over our lives when we aren't fully present. Depression is just like that old man who insulted my shoes. When the self-defeating narratives and thoughts of depression take over, we get swept up in overwhelming feelings that we are unworthy and unsafe, so we begin to unconsciously react.

Presence, mindfulness, and consciousness are tools we can use to notice when we begin to slide down those paths and reconnect with our power. Like the toaster and the panic attack, we have the freedom to decide what is real or not.

Depression and anxiety have no power over us if we are in the present moment, fully accepting what is happening and not resisting. We just have to keep coming back and reminding ourselves, I write my own story, depression doesn't.

Presence Is a Practice

The good news is that presence and mindfulness are practices, like weightlifting or playing guitar. There is nothing mystical or sexy about it. It's a lifelong practice and craft. We never arrive or figure it out, but the more we tune in, the better and easier it gets.

Some days it will be easy to find presence; some days it will be the hardest thing you've ever done. There's a saying in yoga that goes, "Every time you sit down to do yoga, it's like the first time you've ever done yoga." Practicing mindfulness is a bit like that too.

We just keep coming back to seeing what is here and now whenever we find ourselves lost. The present moment, our thoughts, our emotions and feelings are changing all the time, every second, every minute. We just keep noticing.

How to Find Presence

The good news is that presence is always a single breath away. At any and every moment of our lives, we can take a deep breath and reconnect with our hearts and spirit, coming back to the here and now.

Anything we do can be a practice in mindfulness and presence. You can make anything you do a prayer or meditation practice. If you catch yourself getting lost in thought, just come back to your breath and sensations in your body and notice what is there without judgment.

Next time you are washing the dishes, notice the texture of the plate and the feeling of the warm water. When eating, notice if you are actually tasting the food you eat. When talking to someone, actually look into their eyes and see them, noticing all the details in their face that make them uniquely them. How does that change your experience?

Again, the power here is that when we are awake in the present moment, focusing on a taste, a sound, a smell, we are not lost in the narrative of depression. We are either present, or we are lost in story and suffering. We can't exist in both.

We are retraining our minds, hearts, and spirits to be

here now, not lost in mental despair. We cannot coexist in those spaces simultaneously. We cannot feel both fear and gratitude at the same time.

And if we do feel despair, we feel it deeply and fully and don't run from it.

Presence is flow. It doesn't force anything. If we do make mistakes, lose presence, or act out, we notice that too. Do we beat ourselves up? Are we kind to ourselves? It makes life a game of watching, noticing, and being. Remember S.A.L.

What Grounds You?

A good way to find presence is to ask yourself the following questions:

- What does grounding mean to you?
- What gets you out of your head and into your heart and body?
- What brings you back to presence?
- What helps you lose yourself in flow?

Dance, yoga, writing songs, or playing the piano help ground me. If you can't think of something, ask yourself, what is an activity I never regret doing?

To suss out what works for me, I ask myself the question, does it bring me closer to God or further from God? God = being and presence. Here are some additional ways to come back to the present moment.

Breath

I've mentioned this a lot already, but breath is one of the best ways to get present. At any and every moment of our lives, we can connect back with our source and take a deep breath and remember that we are safe and we are loved. Throughout the day, you can pause to take a deep breath and notice how you are feeling.

Meditation

I recommend starting a daily meditation practice. Try it in the morning before you start your day. Start with ten minutes, just sitting down and noticing your breath, thoughts, and sensations. If thoughts come up, notice them and your reactions, and come back to your breath. Apps like Headspace and Calm are great for beginning meditators.

In my bullet journal, I have two lists. One is things that bring me closer to the present moment, and the other is things that take me away. I also have a list of what trashes my presence and can lead to rocky mental health moments for me.

Here is a list of ways I reconnect with the present moment. Find something fun that serves you.

- Large stretches of time away from my phone
- Yoga: a practice of moving meditation

- Exercise: I like running because I focus on taking deep breaths
- Music: songwriting, playing piano or guitar, listening to music
- Breath work: holotropic is a form I enjoy
- Time in nature: hikes, beach walks
- Prayer
- Writing and journaling

Here are the things that pull me away from the present moment:

- Video games
- Putting pressure on myself
- Violent movies and depressing TV shows
- Fragmenting my focus
- Porn
- Social media and the internet
- Time with people who don't serve me
- Saying yes to things I should have said no to
- Fast food, unhealthy fried food, sugar, caffeine, alcohol, drugs
- People who don't see me, who I don't feel safe around
- Not sleeping

Ways to Integrate This Chapter

- Anytime you are mentally down, practice asking yourself, "What am I resisting?" Keep naming answers until you peel back the layers to reveal the root of what you're feeling. Then ask, "How could I best serve and take care of myself?" Listen for an answer and give yourself the grace and compassion to take aims to help yourself.

- Start a meditation routine in the morning before your day starts. Download Calm, Insight Timer, or Headspace, or find a Tara Brach meditation on YouTube.

- Make something you do already a meditation. Washing the dishes. Watering plants. Doing laundry. Tasting food. Make the decision to be fully present with whatever you are doing. Notice all the sensations, the feelings. If you catch yourself drifting away with thoughts, just come right back to the feelings and sensations of the moment. The sun on your face, the wetness of the clothes. The sound they make when you hang them on the rack. Put away your phone for this.

- Try something this week that puts you in your physical body. Dancing, surfing, running, singing, yoga, etc.

- Write your own lists of activities that bring you to presence and activities that take you away from presence.

- Practice S.A.L. in any situation where you feel you are resisting, whether it's with another person or with yourself.
- Start to notice how you feel after certain activities or with people. Is it draining or fulfilling? Does it bring you to presence or take you away? Check in with yourself multiple times a day. After talking with a friend, after exercising.

Chapter Eight:

IDENTITY
Of Gods and Karens

My band was due onstage in five minutes, and as usual, we were shattering every cool stereotype of what a rock band does before going on stage. Instead of making out with hot girls and doing cocaine, my bass player and I were both sprinting to find the goddamn porta potties on maze-like festival grounds to take last-minute poops and nervously pee so we wouldn't have to play a whole show with the added weight of, well, you know.

We were about to play a radio festival for one of the biggest rock stations in the country, and I had just peeked around the outdoor stage to see the crowd: a sea of forty thousand people. My reaction was both nervous excitement and, oh God, I have to poop.

In five minutes, the radio DJ host, sounding more like a professional wrestling announcer, will call out our band name with a yell and we will perform our songs, walking on stage like legends and forgetting that we were just in a humid porta potty praying to God for something to come out.

The closest I've ever felt to being a god was playing shows like this. For a certain amount of time, displayed on a little red LED clock stage right, no one on the planet can tell you what to do. For thirty minutes, you are God. The stage is yours. Do whatever the hell you want with the microphone.

It's one of the biggest power trips ever. Your image is projected onto multistory jumbotrons. Your voice is like Zeus echoing out from the sky, projected out from a two-story-tall speaker system.

I remember one set, I saw a kid wearing a Muppet hat, and I told the audience I wanted the hat. They lifted him up, crowd surfed him to the stage, and handed me the hat. It was both horrifying and awesome because I got a quick taste of power and how quickly people will bend to your will if you have a guitar and a microphone.

As a rock band starting out, we would pray for these shows because they were so much fun. We were treated like kings. We'd get gift bags. There was catering. You got shiny backstage passes. Interns carried your gear and drove you around on golf carts. The station would play your song and do interviews with you. We got to play with some of our idols on these bills. I felt like a big deal.

We loved the shows because we were still a fledging band. We didn't have a big draw in a lot of cities, so these shows meant you were guaranteed to play in front of a huge crowd.

When we toured, we would play these types of shows in between selling dozens of tickets in other cities and then be reminded that we were a band just starting out with a fledging fanbase. These festival sets would lift us up . . . but then they would end up reminding me of everything I wasn't yet.

We'd finish the show and then be back in the hotel room, sleeping two grown men to a bed. I'd wait for my turn to get high in the shower and jerk off while waiting for my other bandmates to finish jerking off in the shower, yet no one acts or admits to actually jerking off in the shower. They said, "Oh, I just like to steam and exfoliate my skin after shows," as they walk out, phone in hand, porn still on the unlocked screen.

Then you get four hours of sleep, and the next day you're back in the twelve-passenger van that would make a garbage can seem like a spa, driving ten hours to play the next show, which couldn't be more different than the festival you played yesterday.

You arrive at a bar to play a set for nine people on a Tuesday night in a town that's most famous for its pig wrestling. No one helps you carry your gear. Instead of having a barrier between you and the crowd or that elusive and coveted backstage pass in a festival with tens of thousands of people, there is no one to separate you from the drunk sixty-five-year-old who accosts you for an hour after the show about your guitar pickups, while you watch the cute girls at the bar get bored and leave. Before you know it, you are jerking off in the shower again, wondering what the fuck is happening and how you got here. This was the real ego trip of touring. You never knew what you were going to show up to.

Up until I was twenty-eight, I derived my entire identity and sense of self-worth from being "the lead singer of a rock band." I only identified with all things worldly. I fell face-first into the trap of placing my entire sense of self and worth in external things: achievements, praise, and circumstances. This was painful as hell. Life in a touring rock band was especially painful for my ego because of these frequent, juxtaposing messages of "I'm a big deal" and "I'm a small deal."

If we got a tour, I felt worthy of life. If we played one of these festivals, I felt invincible, godlike, and immortal. If I wrote a good song, I was a good person. If we got radio play, I mattered.

On the other hand, if we didn't get a tour, I was worthless. If we played a bar for three people, I felt like a failure and thought it meant that me and my art were worthless. If I wrote a bad song, I was talentless. If I played a bad show, I drowned in shame, guilt, and self-hatred and wanted to kill myself. If we didn't get the blog write-up, or not enough people liked the post about our song release, my life didn't matter, and my entire existence felt threatened and meaningless.

Living like this was hell because nothing was ever enough. There was no end. No amount of external praise was enough to fill the hole I was trying to fill.

There were no amount of songs I could write or money I could make to feel, you know what, now that I made X amount of dollars or hit X amount of followers, I finally mean something. It was chasing highs and dopamine hits in everything external. Looking back, I see it was a losing game. All I did was suffer.

Identity was one of the ways I hid from my depression. I put all my identity into my rock band so I didn't have to be present with the pain I was in. When it was good, it was great, but when it was bad, it was suffocating. My band and music were a vehicle for my identity and a Band-Aid for all my pain.

When my band broke up, I had to face the fact that I had absolutely no idea who I was without it. My entire identity was wrapped up in this project, and when it fell apart, depression bottomed out. I had to go on a journey to rediscover my true identity and figure out who the hell I was without music, without my band.

This chapter is about identity. Who you are and who you are not. Where you source your identity and how you see your place in this world can set you free or cause you to suffer more.

Depression and identity are interwoven. When we forget our identity and our true nature, we suffer. When we place our identity in the wrong things, we suffer. Who depression tells us we are versus who we actually are are two very different things. Whatever you identify yourself with becomes your worth, and if that's not in alignment, it can create problems. When I remembered who I was, I found solace and healing.

Depression Is a Storytelling Liar

Depression is one of the greatest storytellers of all time. In terms of creating alternate realities and worlds within worlds, they could give J.K. Rowling and Tolkien a run for their money.

Depression feeds you stories. Stories about who you are, what you're worth, and your place in this world. Stories about why we are stuck, how we are unworthy, how we are powerless. Stories about our past, our future, people in our life, our place in the world.

Most often these stories are bullshit. As per the last chapter, these stories are derived from thoughts and likely colored with depression's greatest hits: shame, unworthiness, fear, hopelessness, negativity, and limitation.

These stories are dangerous because they not only destroy our sense of self but warp our reality.

Once we are fed enough "I'm unworthy" thoughts, we begin to believe it, and it starts to affect our decision-making. When we make our life decisions from a place of unworthiness, it probably doesn't lead to a big, happy, open life.

Believing these stories takes our identity hostage and blinds us to our true nature. We start to see the world differently, start to see our identity differently, and start to lose all of our power. When we believe the stories of depression and anxiety, we give them all of our power.

I believed everything depression told me without a fight. When it told me I was meaningless, I believed it. It shaped how I saw my identity in this world and universe. I believed I was a meaningless mistake and the worst person on the planet.

Echoing the last chapters on thoughts and presence, we should take a close look at what depression is saying to us. How is it talking to us? Is it the truth?

Again, the best way to identify the stories is using presence. What are the stories depression is telling about you? Who is depression telling you you are?

Where Do You Get Your Identity?

External or Internal

Another question no one has probably asked you is: Where do you get your identity from? Is it sustainable? Do you get it from external things such as money, wealth, jobs, follower count, family, or heritage? Or is it from an internal place such as knowing you are spirit incarnate having a human experience, or identifying with values or character?

Whatever we place importance on, consciously or unconsciously, becomes a part of who we are and how we see ourselves in this world. This either sets us free or terrorizes us. We live and die by the sword of wherever we source our identity.

When we look for worth and identity in external things, the chase never ends. There is never enough.

If you get your identity from your follower count and likes, there is always someone who has more. If you get your identity from productivity, when have you done enough to be worthy or rest? If you get your identity from fame, you are beholden to a vicious cycle of ups and downs. If you get your identity from having money, when you don't have it, you might feel unworthy.

While working on this chapter, a friend told me her sister-in-law killed herself. She was a big-time lawyer and lost her fortune during the pandemic. She couldn't see herself without money and thought her money problems were unfixable. When you place your identity in wealth, and that wealth disappears, who are you?

If your job or social standing was taken away, would you be ok with who and what was left?

Placing identity and worth in external things is building

an empire inside a sandcastle. None of it will last. Money, family, relationships, friends, and fame all come and go. If we look for a solid foundation in temporary, ever-changing things, it becomes an emotional roller coaster and a losing game.

I'm not saying it's bad to feel pride or joy or find meaning in these things. Playing these roles and celebrating the joy they bring is an integral part of the human experience. And that's what they are. Roles. My point is, when we place our entire self-worth and identity in these things, it can be a recipe for disaster.

It is essential in healing depression to genuinely ask yourself the question, where do I get my sense of self from? How do I identify my role as a human on this planet? It's a good question to examine your belief system and system of worthiness as well.

You are not your job. You are not your follower count. You are not your fame level. You are not your productivity. You are not your bank account balance. You are not your height, your weight, or your education. You are not only your depression.

Also, rest in the fact that you are enough simply because you exist. Rest in the knowledge that your being born is validation enough that you are worthy of this life, of love, of happiness. Beyond all the expectations of society, just the fact that you are alive is a miracle enough. You matter.

Internally Sourcing Identity

If looking for identity outside of ourselves leads to suffering, it means we have to take the journey within. Sourcing your identity internally means you base your self-worth on what's within, not outside. Intentions, spirit, knowing, soul, values, faith, and character are examples of what lies within that you can draw upon to source your worth.

The question I've found most helpful for internally sourcing a healthy sense of self is, What are the values, qualities, or truths about yourself no one can take away?

If you lost everything, what are the things about yourself you could find solace in? You can't lose integrity or honesty when you go bankrupt. And if you don't know, what a beautiful journey you are about to take to get to know yourself.

Sourcing identity in this way builds a deeper and stronger foundation than when we look outside for answers. We are less bothered by the world and outcomes because we know who we are at the core of our being. A deep inner knowing of self is also helpful for building a strong foundation.

Reading spiritual texts, talk therapy, and sitting with plant medicine have been the most helpful resources in sourcing my identity in a healthy way. The more I ask the question, What does it mean to be a human and who am I? the more I identify with inner solace versus external grasping.

God and Animal, Human and Spirit

Being a human is tough. No one really tells you how to do this, who we actually are, or what we are made out of. There are a lot of layers to life, and in those layers, there are so many ways for us to find identity and also suffer.

We have to deal with the ego-layer questions of "How do I make this spreadsheet?" and "Am I good at kissing?" And we must meet the big existential questions that stress me out and make me want to throw up, like "What is consciousness, and what's behind it?" "What comes after death?" and "Who even are we, where do we come from, and what do we do with this life thing?"

Echoing the last section, if we take what society tells us at face value about who we should be and who we are, it's likely we will find our identity in everything external: money, fame, legacy, profession, relationships.

But if we peek behind the curtain, we will realize this is only part of the story.

We as humans are in this weird predicament of being both spirit and human. We are gods and goddesses, composed of infinite spirit and power, pure consciousness and bliss, who at the same time have to pay rent, go to our nephew's god-awful piano rehearsals, and sit on the phone with the IRS discussing the sheer absurdity of tax laws. (Who even made this shit?)

Every person walking in this world is made of God and spirit, the source material of everything, but most forget this and are asleep to their power and true self, getting caught up in world drama and believing everything their mind thinks.

We are both of this planet and not of this planet. God and animal. Divine and human. Spirit and human. We forget we are divinity incarnate, walking around eating sandwiches, looking at our phones and trying to find porn.

The humanness of our lives, our work, vocation, and relationships is amazing to be a part of. But it can be hard to navigate those things by themselves when we lose sense and remembrance of our sacred nature.

When I forget about my divine nature, I suffer. When I get caught up in human drama and stressed and anxious about how things will work out, I suffer. The further I get from knowing my true nature and dignity, the more I suffer. The closer I get to that identity, the more I fall in love with life, enjoy it, and live in presence.

Bufo

Psychedelics have been the most powerful tools in shifting my identity from human to spirit and remembering who I really am. They have opened my lens wider to who we really are and what we are made of. In terms of depression, remembering my true identity has been one of the biggest reliefs and healings.

One of the most life-changing experiences I've ever had was a half hour with the secretion of a Sonoran toad, otherwise called Bufo.

I sat on a mat listening to new-age music in the background while the shaman saged my entire body. She then sat across from me and took out a glass pipe (looking a bit too much like a crack pipe for my liking) and a sippy cup (a plastic cup with a plastic top that looks like a misshapen condom with a straw sticking out to keep the vapor in) and instructed me to breathe with her. As I deeply inhaled three to four times, she lit the cup, put the straw in my mouth, and instructed me to inhale the smoke with all of my might and hold my breath as long as I could.

In just enough time to have the thought, "Is this working? Oh my God, what if this doesn't work? I spent three hundred dollars," I exhaled and coughed. Without a choice, I fell back on the mat behind me and blacked out, reality dissolving in an instant. At this point, everyone's experience is totally different, so I can only speak to my own.

I experienced Source, God, Universal Intelligence. This medicine plunged me right back to the source of all creation and all being. On this medicine, I came home to a place of oneness.

These places can be referred to as non-dual planes of consciousness. A non-dual realm is a place beyond duality. Earth, in all of its material and physical existence, is a place of duality. Duality is when opposites exist together: male and female, good and bad, hot and cold, Backstreet Boys and NSYNC.

These are landscapes of an infinite nature. Places with

no end or beginning. Places of infinite expansion and eternal boundlessness. You get to hang and merge back into the source of all creation, the source of all being. The place where we all come from and will all return to. The void.

You are right back in the cosmic soup, being with the material and energy that makes up every living being on the planet. This is the power and space between every cell, the power that created every cell, the force that gave birth to the macrocosm of the entire universe.

And the thing about this energy, this limitless consciousness, this power, is that it's pure love, pure bliss, and total joy, and it goes on forever. It's heaven. You get to bask in, experience, and remember infinite, boundless places of pure being, endless streams of love, and eternal, pure, loving awareness of which everything is composed. Hindus call it Atman, capital S Self.

The wild thing about these places is that they are beyond your mind. It's so beyond any sort of human rationality that none of our language, thoughts, or cleverness can hang here. These are realms of limitlessness, and by nature, normal human cognition only limits it. You can't think your way in or out of it; you have to open your heart and experience it. Your rational mind can't hang because it's not a place of doing; it's a place of being. The kicker is, how often do we get to go to a place where there is no thinking, no monkey mind, only pure being and witnessing? It's usually a place where there is everything or nothing, and "place" isn't the right word at all because that implies you're going some-where, and if it's neither everywhere nor nowhere, where can it really be?

What's most miraculous about these planes is that they are planes of being, not doing. To quote Paul Chek speaking on non-duality in an interview: "There is nothing happen-ing here but everything," or everything happening here but nothing. There's nothing to be here but everything. There's everything to do but nothing. In these places, there is noth-ing to gain, nothing to lose, nothing to achieve, nowhere to be, nothing to stress or worry about, and nothing to fear. The witness consciousness just watches it all.

Because literally everything is here, it's a place of true abundance. Duality paradigms that produce notions like "enough" and "lack" don't exist because it's everything, all the time, everywhere. Yes, it can sound like a paradox, but remember, we are talking of places beyond language and rationality.

Some people find this terrifying because spending time (although time doesn't exist here either) in these places is essentially a death rehearsal. You visit realms beyond everything, where there is no more earth, no possessions, no depression, no Kyle, mind, no thoughts, no dreams or anxi-ety of writing or finishing this book, no shitty boss, or nine to five, no goals, no exes blowing up your phone demanding their clothes back.

You, as an ego, or a material physical entity or identity,

do not exist anymore. It's an ego death of the highest order. Both times, driving to Bufo ceremonies, I was horrified to the point of panic, blasting Songs for the Deaf, clutching my steering wheel with my heart pounding out of my chest from terror. My brain screams, "We could have just gotten ice cream, motherfucker, but no you need to go practice your own death on a Tuesday morning."

The whole kicker is that the experience itself only lasts twenty to forty minutes. But when you're in those places of non-duality, time doesn't exist; a second and infinity are somehow the same thing.

When I came to, the plane of reality and the room I was in came back into focus. I looked up and saw the shaman smiling at me, playing sound bowls. Every time I was left thinking, "What the hell just happened?" and "I can't believe I thought I was ok before that." Before I knew it, I was back in my car, driving down the Malibu coastline on Pacific Coast Highway, staring at a traffic light and thinking, "I'm so glad I didn't go bowling today."

For me, these ceremonies are meditations on identity. They are the most humbling and awe-inspiring experiences of my entire life because they remind me of who I am and where I come from. They remind me I am an undying and unchanging spirit whose nature is boundless—infinite spirit and eternal bliss.

This entire experience is more of a coming back home to Source. And boy, are we made out of powerful stuff.

These experiences changed my concept and sense of self. Yes, I may be Kyle Michael Nicolaides, who writes songs or isn't making a lot of money right now, but I am also a changeless, undying spirit composed of the same matter that created this entire universe. This changed my narrative of depression forever.

When it comes to identity, I believe this is who we are.

Ways To Integrate This Chapter

- *Journal Prompt:* Write about where you get your identity from. Who are you? What are the roles you are playing? Is it serving you? Where do you get your sense of self from? Is it sustainable? Healthy?
- Write three stories or narratives that depression is telling you about your identity and about your life. Then rewrite those stories and narratives in a positive and empowering way.
- Begin to source your identity internally. Write down values, qualities, character traits, and intentions that no one can take away from you. Write out what it means to you and what it would look like to embody those traits.

Chapter Nine:

LIVING IN ALIGNMENT
A Life Inventory

Being in a vocal booth is like being in a stand-up coffin. You're in a fourteen-feet by fourteen-feet room with no windows and no air conditioning, and it's just you, alone with your voice, the thoughts in your head, and a microphone. People in another room chime in through your headphones like ghostly voices coming to you from outer space to give you feedback, usually "Your pitch is flat," "Do you need a bump of coke?" or "Maybe a toothy blowjob will fix your fast phrasing there, cowboy." Once I got feedback that was different from the rest, that was a game changer.

I was in the vocal booth, which in this case was also a laundry room, fifteen minutes into singing a song for my band's second record, when the producer stopped me. I heard silence in my headphones as she paused, trying to figure out what to say, and when she did, it went something like this: "When you sing, it sounds blank, like no one is there. It sounds like you're beneath or behind something. There's no passion or emotion. You sound numb."

I immediately knew exactly what she was talking about and why. I wasn't even shocked. I was surprised at how apparent it was to her; I thought I was hiding it better.

This was during my full-blown depression denial period when the only coping mechanism I had was to run, hide, and go numb.

I thought that if I could hide from my life in other people or things, putting all my focus into outer places, then I wouldn't have the time, space, or energy to look at my own life. If I didn't have to look at myself, then I wouldn't have to sit with the emptiness, pain, fear, and despair that depression was creating. Therefore I wouldn't have to admit how broken or sad I really was; that the heaviness and sorrow lurking down below wasn't really there or real. It was numbing, self-preservation.

So I closed off my heart and looked for places to hide. I entered a relationship I didn't want to be in. I wrote and recorded an album for the wrong reasons. I was living somewhere that didn't fulfill me. I trusted other people's ideas for my life instead of listening to my soul's yearning. I stayed in a band I didn't want to be in because other people told me I was great at it. My friend group was less than stellar.

I thought this was working pretty well, until it became glaringly clear that my D.I.Y. coping mechanism for depression had spectacularly backfired in ways I didn't anticipate. It had made everything worse.

Life felt like death. The energetic cost of living a life out of integrity and alignment worsened my depression. I wasn't living a life that was truly mine. I was living an artificial, inauthentic existence, a life within a life. I'd built myself a prison.

I wasn't following my heart, wasn't trusting myself, wasn't being seen. None of my needs were being met, and as a result, my anxiety and depression got worse. I spun out even more. In trying to avoid the sorrow and pain in my life, I'd numbed out all of the joy, happiness, and light.

When it came to being in the studio and hearing those words from the producer, I fully realized how spectacularly my plan had backfired and how it was affecting me in ways I never could have planned.

The whole point of this chapter is to show you how to live in alignment and authenticity. Are you living your truth and a life that is honestly and authentically yours? Are your daily actions and work in alignment with your deepest purpose and truth?

Spending time with the wrong people, doing what other people think you should do, and ignoring your purpose or passion can create fertile breeding grounds for depression and anxiety.

The self-care chapter was all about taking care of your heart, spirit, and body; this chapter is about taking a life inventory—taking a look at your life to find what isn't serving you and then asking, How might you take ownership and responsibility to make changes that could help alleviate your depression?

This chapter will remind you of your power and sovereignty. I want you to know that every single moment of your life, you are always in your power to change what you can control. This chapter will also teach you how to take steps to live in alignment (i.e., to live in all of your truth and brilliant authenticity).

What Is Living in Alignment?

So what is living a life in alignment and authenticity?

The simple answer is living an open and honest life that is purposeful to you. It's living your life, not what someone else thinks your life should be. Chasing goals that are yours and not other people's goals for you. It's being honest with your heart's agenda and your unique intentions for this life and then following and acting on that wisdom. It's when you feel purpose in your work, your relationships, and your life.

It's doing things for the right reasons. It's letting go of what doesn't serve you or make you happy. It's having the bravery to sit with yourself and be honest about who you are and what you want, then going for it.

Living Out of Alignment

Living out of alignment is not living in and expressing your deepest truth, purpose, who you really are, and why you are really here. It's settling and making decisions from fear, scarcity, and lack. It's working jobs that don't fulfill you or bring you purpose or being in any relationship—business, friendship, or romantic—that doesn't serve you. It's when we try to live up to others' expectations of who they think we are rather than who we really are.

Living out of alignment is a breeding ground for unhappiness and depression because we can feel trapped in our own lives as victims, living a "life in layers." Living a life in layers is when we are not living in our truth but hiding and covering the truth up behind other things.

Here's the thing. You can lie to your friends, family, even yourself, but you cannot lie to your spirit. You can fake it all you want, but if you're not living in alignment, your soul, heart, and spirit know. The truth is, you actually can't fake it.

As much as our minds like to think they know what's happening, our bodies have even greater intelligence. Your body knows when you're in a situation you shouldn't be in. Pay attention to your body language, the feelings inside, the tone of your voice, your energy, and the energy field around you when you're around someone you shouldn't be with.

However clever your mind thinks it is, it will never outsmart the wisdom of the soul because it communicates through the body when it senses misalignment.

Also, remember to think of yourself like gumbo. Everything affects you. Having a job that kills you or a toxic relationship will affect your mental health. Going to school or doing something because someone else thinks that is what you want when you know it goes against your truth can make depression flare up. Depression (and anxiety) can be like an indicator light to alert you when you are out of alignment.

You Are Always in Your Power

After my band broke up, I still owed my record label one more album, and I had no clue what to do. I had no direction for my life, let alone music, and was more focused on surviving another day than trying to be a rock star.

There was one person at my label who was essentially the gatekeeper of my creativity. He was the biggest voice and opinion on which of my songs would be released. I got caught in a full-blown victim mentality with him.

I'd write dozens of songs, send them to him, get vague or little to no feedback and then spiral out. I thought nothing I wrote was good enough for him, and I spun a false narrative about how he hated me and was a malicious dictator trying to wreck my life. I felt powerless because I couldn't get my songs out in the world, and it spawned resentment, anger, and hatred toward myself and this other person for being stuck in this creative limbo-purgatory.

Instead of thinking about how I could take control of the situation and be assertive, I got lost in depression narratives, which had put my life in a cruel stasis and holding pattern. A year or two later, I managed to slug through and deliver seven songs of the ten I owed them.

I look back now and realize I could have easily vocalized to him how I felt, but depression had me tied in so much unworthiness and so many mental knots that I created a whole other world of pessimism and fear. Depression made it hard for me to believe I was someone worthy of standing up for myself or that there'd be any kind of positive outcome for doing so.

One morning I was cleaning house and found an original copy of my record deal. When I started reading it, my jaw dropped. I wanted to both cry and vomit. Teenage me had specifically fought for the clause that I retain one hundred percent full creative control regarding releases. Twenty-seven-year-old Kyle had realized how badly he'd forgotten his own power.

I had access to power and control all along, yet because of depression, low self-worth, and fear, I had completely given them away to someone else.

As soon as I read that, I decided to take back my power fully and finish the record deal, sending them three songs

I loved. The deal was finished, and it felt like I was taking back my creativity and my life.

Aren't most of us with depression in this situation? We forget how much power we have because of the depression narratives in our heads. We give our power to other people and situations and then feel victimized because of it. We don't feel worthy of goodness, so we give our lives and power to other people.

The biggest truth that depression wants you to forget is that, at any moment, at any given time in our lives, we are always standing strong in our power.

Now, forever, and always, every single moment, we have the power, we have the freedom, and we are in charge of making any decision, taking any action we want.

Power isn't force or domination; it's the ability to act freely and consciously in any given moment. We are free to act, free to think, free to do literally anything with our lives at any given moment when we consciously choose to do so.

We are never trapped. We are always in control of our own lives. Anything else is a story or an excuse. It's like we've locked ourselves in a jail cell and forgot that the key has been in our hands the whole time.

Our brains complicate things with stories that often leave us as powerless victims. Depression turns everyone into monsters out to get us. Depression limits you, makes you think everything is hopeless and there are no options.

The truth is, there's always an option and a choice to be made. There's always something you can do, despite your mind insisting you are stuck. Sometimes depression makes that hard to see, but it's always there. There is always some action or perspective shift.

At any point, we can change careers, start taking antidepressants, make a big change, leave a partner, sell everything we own and start over. Yes, there are consequences to every action, and there are also big consequences to inaction. Worst-case scenario, there's almost no situation that can't be amended. Baby steps or a simple mental shift are better than no action.

Most times, the only thing that's stopping us is the stories in our heads that depression and anxiety weave. The forces that keep real change from happening in our life are psychic, not external. It's those fear-based wars in our own heads that keep us stuck, not the actual circumstances in our life. We aren't thinking creatively enough because depression and anxiety have limited our possibilities.

Then when we don't act, it creates more anxiety and more depression.

Yes, I'm sure you're thinking it's way more complicated than that, but it's also not. You can keep your excuses.

The questions remain: How long are we willing to put up with not living in alignment? How much pain can we take before it becomes unbearable and we have to act?

Depression and Strength

One of the dumbest misconceptions I've ever heard about people with depression is that they are weak and lazy. This is bullshit. People with depression are some of the strongest people on the planet.

Life is already hard enough without having a brain that is hell-bent on self-annihilation at all times. People with depression are not only dealing with the pressures of real life but also the mental apocalypse in their heads 24/7.

The sheer strength, will, and determination of anyone who lives day in and day out with depression is mind-blowing. To show up in any capacity—while behind the scenes you have thoughts that are attacking you, low energy, brain fog, deep sadness, and the urge to cry all the time—is a superpower. If that doesn't scream strength, I don't know what does.

You are playing the video game of life on Extra Hard Sudden Death Mode while blindfolded with frostbitten fingers. You're running a marathon with a two-hundred-pound weight on your back.

I know you probably don't feel strong because of all the ways depression is showing up, but just for surviving, getting through the day to day, showing up even when you feel terrible, and doing your best even when your brain says it's nothing, I think you are a superhero.

I believe that if you can live for extended periods of

time with depression, you can do anything. If you can endure the sheer brutality of day in and day out depression, you can not only come out of it and find healing but create the life of your dreams. If you can overcome the beast that's taken up residence in your being, you can overcome anything. Depression is not weakness; it is unimaginable strength.

The reason I'm bringing this up is that I want you to know that you are more than capable of living fully in your power and authenticity. You have the strength to live the life of your dreams.

Radical Responsibility

When I was a teenager, I found a Maya Angelou quote in a fortune cookie. It was so profound that I taped it to the odometer panel on my stallion of a '98 White VW Golf so I could see it every day. It read: "If you don't like something in your life, change it. If you can't change it, change your attitude."

I mean, if anything sums up how to do life, it's that sentence. Anything and everything you are up against can come back to this simple one-two punch of a quote.

I like it because it's empowering. It empowers you to take responsibility and ownership either for the events in your life or how you see them. No blame, no excuses, no stories. All responsibility.

It also invokes action. Are you going to take action on

whatever it is you don't like, change it or your perception of it, or not? If you don't do anything about it, you can't complain.

Did I follow her advice? No, of course not. We sold the car, and along with it, the message got lost. I got swept up in the wave of victimhood, helplessness, and paralyzing terror of depression and anxiety for the next ten years. My point now is, you don't have to fall into the same pits I did. That's the purpose of this section.

The good news, as Maya Angelou's quote above reminds us, is that at all times in our lives, we have two options: change it or change our attitude about it. When talking about depression, this quote matters. Untie the knots where we can untie the knots, and if we can't untie, change the story around the knot.

We already know that depression closes off possibilities and can make it hard to think of positive outcomes. This is why radical responsibility is so important. I want you to be aware of this so you can start to change it.

There are rarely, I want to again state, rarely, situations that are so doomed, so seemingly permanent that we can't change them or get out of them. Not a lot of decisions or things in this life are beyond repair. There is always a choice to be had, an action to be taken, or a different way to look at the situation. Most times, you can't see it because you're looking in the wrong place or your perspective is limited because of depression. Another chapter throwback, this is why it's so important to speak about your mental health with other people. They can help you see your situation differently.

Also, if you don't know what to do, use this as the perfect opportunity to begin to trust the universe. Use it as a reason to change your energy. You can turn a situation you don't like into a catalyst for change.

We get locked into grooves, habits, and patterns and forget that at any moment, we can blow everything up and change. The only ceilings we have are the ones under which we limit ourselves. In the present moment, we are limitless possibilities, and we are eternal. It's when we start to tell ourselves stories about why we can't do things, or how hard it might be, or make excuses or play the victim that we take an endless sky of possibility and spirit and place it into an airless box that we hold in our hands, and limit God, the universe, and spirit from working its magic.

If your excuse is, "I can't think of any actions or mindset shifts for this," it's a great time to get resourceful, research, and learn what other people did in your situation. Ask for help or read ways to expand your consciousness so you have new coping mechanisms and new tools to react. Take action, or change your attitude.

We're either living small and limited, decorating the jail cell we've designed for our life, or reaching into the ever-expansiveness of spirit and the unknown, and I believe this is a conscious choice we make daily.

As I've said before, life is all about flow. There is a flow to everything, and it's either open or closed. When we aren't living in alignment, living our truth, the flow becomes stagnant. We're blocking energy in all kinds of places. Depression loves stagnant energy. Stagnant energy leads to more stagnant energy, which leads to more depression.

When you live like this, it limits what can actually come in and help your life. You're pretty much guaranteeing nothing will change, and then you find yourself in the same washing machine cycle over and over again, and it's hell.

Inventory of Your Life

How do you know if you're living in alignment? Take a life inventory. What Marie Kondo does to your house, this does to your life.

Taking inventory of your life means going through all the categories in your life and checking in on your fulfillment level. This process involves clearing out your life so more light can come in.

Being in an unhealthy romantic relationship or being in a toxic work or living space can wreak havoc on your mental health. Remember, you are gumbo. Everything affects everything. This practice means asking yourself the question, What is poisoning your gumbo, and what are you going to do about it? When we remove the energetic blocks in our life, depression doesn't have as much space to breathe.

Also, I want to stress that when you do this practice, intend to write, speak, and listen from your heart and gut. Try to do this from a calm and grounded place, tapping into your intuition. Make it a date with yourself. Tap into your inner truth and knowing when you write this.

1. Rate It

Write these out, and for every category give yourself an honest rating of 1–10 on how fulfilled you are.

Living Situation: Apartment/home, city, state

Romantic Relationship(s)

Friends

Job, Vocation, or School

Income and Finances

Social and Community Life

Spiritual Life

Hobbies

Free Time

Leisure

Family

Body

Food

Movement

2. Deep Dive

When you've done this, look at the list. Don't panic if all the numbers are low. This is actually a great thing.

When you find an item list that scored low, write out everything you're unhappy about with it. Get specific.

Maybe you're going to college because your parents want you to, and you always knew there was a different path for you. Maybe you think you need this job for some reason, even though it sucks out your soul. Maybe you're not living where you want to live, whether that's an apartment, home, city, or country.

When you find something that doesn't serve you, ask:

- How might this be contributing to my depression?
- What do I gain from being stuck in this pattern? That is, what do I have to gain by not making a change to this?
- Am I living my full truth in this situation, or living according to what others are expecting of me?
- What would I do in this situation if I were fearless?
- What am I grateful for in this situation? (Even if it's not serving you right now, there might be things about it you can be grateful for. It's a lot easier to change when we come from a place of thank you than fuck off.)

Doing inventory is interesting because it allows you to see a clear glimpse of your belief systems. Why are you staying in something you shouldn't be? What's the belief underneath? Is there a hidden belief grounded in unworthiness or fear?

When you look at your list and find something that isn't serving you, spend time with it and try to get the core issue. What is really going on here?

If your best friend bitches and complains all the time and has no space for you, what's beneath that? Maybe you don't feel safe or feel worthy of being seen, so you attract people who affirm that. Try to find the core issue and honor that. Then you can start to change things from that place.

Try to go beyond blaming the other person or situation and go inside of yourself. What is the core of what you deeply feel? How does this situation make you feel? Own what you feel and what doesn't thrill you about the situation.

3. Smallest Action Possible

Now is the fun and empowering part. You get to decide how you move through this. The most important thing is to take action, so go for it.

What actions can I personally take to alleviate this situation or change it to take my power back?

After you spend time with that, write out a super simple and easy action you can take to make the situation better, be it a mental shift or actual action. Even if it's the smallest action ever, it's a step in the right direction. Remember, everything matters with depression.

Maybe it's quitting your job. Maybe it's shifting your mindset. Maybe it's leaving a relationship that doesn't serve you. Maybe it's moving to an apartment with a backyard or buying a goldfish. Maybe it's making a new group of friends. Maybe it's telling someone how you feel and setting a boundary. Maybe it's as simple as decorating your living space with new flowers and a day bed.

If it's a mindset shift, try the question, How can I see this situation differently and approach it in a new light?

Say you know you need to change your living situation. Small steps could be looking at apartment listings, writing about your dream living situation, or driving through neighborhoods to check out houses.

Remember, the way you climb a ladder is one step at a time. Take things in small, manageable steps. Just as you don't clean a house by throwing every possession on the front lawn, you don't need to throw your entire life into upheaval; just start small. Small actionable steps—the next right action—can break down huge daunting goals into manageable bite-sized pieces.

4. Additional Questions and Room to Not Know

Overall, the questions you could ask yourself are:

- What would you need to change in your life to be excited about your future?
- What would it take for you to look forward to things?

Allowing room for not knowing is fine too. You might not know the right action to take. In this case, you might practice willingness. I am willing to experience this differently. I am willing to discover the changes I need in this area of my life. I am willing to align with my truth in this situation. Notice how this simple mindset move toward willingness begins to open things up for you.

Big Picture Points: What's at Stake

We can look at this process as a practice of listening. It's almost like depression is trying to free us. What in our life isn't working? Where are the knots? With whom or where do I feel most down? Our pain and suffering is a teacher. There is wisdom to our emotions.

Don't be afraid to tear down or destroy things you've built or nurtured if they don't serve you anymore. You're never locked into anything in this life, and nothing is permanent. Go ahead, make a mess, fuck things up. It's better than living a life you don't even want.

When we stay in situations and relationships that are "ehs" because we are afraid, we energetically block the "fuck yeahs!" from coming into our life.

Every heartbeat matters. Every moment matters. Every day you stay stuck in something that doesn't serve you is another day you could be open to finding freedom in a new situation.

You'll make mistakes and fuck up, but the difference is, you'll own them, and at least you failed at something you were passionate about. I'd rather fail at something I am passionate about than win at someone else's game for my life. Plus, there's no such thing as failure, only lessons, and every project guides you to the next.

Again, depression loves stagnant energy. When we shake out our life and the situations in it, our depression can begin to clear up. In little ways, like saying no to hanging out with friends that don't serve you, to big ways, like moving somewhere that inspires you.

Not speaking our truth blocks flow. Being around people who don't serve us blocks flow. Living in the wrong city blocks flow. Living someone else's life blocks flow. Discover what is blocking your flow and step toward removing those obstacles from the river of the life meant for YOU.

When we start to simplify our lives and live in accordance with our hearts and intuition, we welcome openness, a new freedom. It's a practice and a craft. We reclaim power over our lives.

But It's So Scary

This process can be scary. Taking control of your life after feeling powerless for so long is a big leap. Usually what keeps us from making changes in our life is fear. Again, humans love to cling to certainty. Often your brain rationalizes that it's safer to be in known suffering than unknown freedom. But nothing, absolutely nothing, in this life is certain, and whatever we think has certainty is an illusion.

Making changes to your life is leaping into the unknown. Our brains fear and hate the unknown simply because we don't know it yet. Obviously, yes, making big changes to your life can be scary, but it's scarier, more painful, and more deadening not living in your truth (i.e., how you are living right now). Behind fear is always freedom. Practice taking baby steps, and it will get easier. Remember, the known is depression. Healing is the unknown. We need the unknown. The known often brings more suffering than the unknown.

You perhaps rationalize, "It's better to have the certainty of a steady relationship that doesn't serve me than to be alone out in the dating wilderness again." Fear of the unknown keeps us from making changes. Fear of the unknown is certain death. We need to leave behind what we know and step into the great void of possibility.

Because we experience a period of time where things feel the same, maybe inside our relationships, careers, or inner patterns, we can falsely assume things are permanent.

Yet nothing is permanent. Emotions aren't permanent, feelings aren't permanent, and depression especially isn't permanent. Though we don't know how things may change, we can guarantee one thing: It won't be like this forever. Have the courage to jump into the unknown and leave behind anything that doesn't serve you.

Ways to Integrate This Chapter

- Take a Life Inventory. Find anything that might be contributing to your depression or negatively affecting your well-being and take action to change it or your mindset around it.
- Write five areas where you aren't living in your power. Write about small steps and actions that would put you back in your power.
- Write five things in your life that are blocking your flow. Then write an action you could take to unblock each thing.
- Find a support system or accountability buddy for this. A men's or women's group. It's easier to make changes when you have support and encouragement from friends or a group.

Chapter Ten:
SUICIDE
One Day Soon but Not Now

When other kids were planning what to do with their lives after college, my dreams were a bit different. They were talking about getting jobs and traveling. I secretly wished and hoped to get hit by a bus. Or maybe get in a car accident. Not enough to kill me or do serious unrepairable damage, just something gentle enough to knock me into a coma so everything could stop and I could finally get some relief. It was what Western doctors call "passive suicidal ideations." I didn't plan, get specific, attempt anything, or experience the hopeless despair where death feels like the only way out. It was obsessive wishful thinking.

If you have ever been suicidal or had an attempt, I am so glad you are here to read this. I hope this chapter can offer you some solace that you are meant to be here and that you and your life are beautiful gifts.

You Never Know What's Next

Suicide is making the fatalistic and baseless claim that you know what's beyond repair and what isn't. Suicide is like writing a scathing review for a movie you walked out of halfway.

Suicide is like pressing your face up so close to a map of the United States that you can only see Bakersfield and think, "This is all there is? I'm out." Once you stand back and see the entire map, you start to have an entirely different sense of what the country, planet, and life are. But up close, your brain gets so fixated on the shortsighted illusionary promise of pain relief that it forgets the bigger picture.

If we see suicide as an issue of consciousness, it's someone being so caught in their pain that they can't see or think of anything else but that pain. People kill themselves because they are in so much mental pain they think ending their life is the only way out.

Your brain is so lost in negative self-talk and narratives of hopelessness, despair, pain, and suffering that you can't see a way out. It's really hard to envision any sort of positive outcome for your life. Ending your life seems like the only way out. Your brain is just trying to find relief from the pain. Suicide seems like the answer. I don't think anyone wants to consciously kill themselves. I think people just want out of the pain they're in.

Suicide makes the biggest and falsest assumption that you know where your life will take you. You don't. The truth is you have no idea what will happen next in your life. You do not know where you will be in one hour, one day, one week, one month, or one year. You never know what's coming next for you. Tomorrow someone or something could walk into your life and change everything. This is reason enough not to end your life. Your sense that it is hopeless and nothing can change is simply not accurate.

Could your life get any worse? Maybe. But it could also get wildly and breathtakingly more beautiful. Why not just stick around and see what happens? What do you have to lose by staying?

Life is the most beautiful and mystical ride of all time. Life is essentially the greatest movie you will ever see. You might as well try to enjoy and celebrate it in the micro ways you can. You're not even here that long, so why would you rush your exit?

Questions on Suicide

When you say you want to kill yourself, what does that even mean? What and who are you even killing? Is it really yourself that you want to kill, or is it something else? Do you even know what you're killing? Are you killing the human role you're playing? Do you want to kill the witness consciousness behind everything?

If you are thinking of killing yourself, what is it that will actually be over?

What's behind this desire? Hopelessness? Do you think you wrecked your life beyond repair?

I think the better question is, What do you want to stop? And what do you want to change? Do you really want to end your life, or do you just want your pain to stop? Do you just want change, or your ego to die, or a different way of being?

Wanting suffering and pain to stop is different than not wanting to be alive. Decouple the pain from the strategy. It's not the strategy you want (suicide); it's the solution to your pain. Suicide is not the solution to your pain that depression says it is. Your reoccurring thought or belief that you don't deserve to be alive is not empirical truth.

The Stories Behind Suicide

Suicide is believing depression narratives above all else and acting on them. There are always stories behind suicide. You don't think you have a future, you think you fucked up your past, and you're in this sort of beyond-redemption state. You think you're unworthy of life. The notion that people would be "better off if I was gone" is trash. I promise you, no matter how annoying you think your existence or life is, it's better to be here than to be gone.

Maybe you're facing a problem. A major life event, some huge financial burden, divorce, or death. Throwback to Chapter 1, I thought my depression was the worst thing to ever happen to me until I realized it was my greatest gift. You also have no idea if whatever problem you are dealing with right now is a good or bad thing. Suicide is only one answer out of a billion possible outcomes.

I guarantee you that whatever problem you are fixated on and want to kill yourself over is fixable. There's a saying: Suicide is a permanent solution to a temporary problem. Your brain right now is overwhelmed and can't rationally think of a solution other than death. If Vince Neil can start a tequila company after killing a man drunk driving, you can move through anything you're facing and come out better. Most everything can be fixed, healed, or changed except you killing yourself.

Do anything and everything you can to get your brain right, then you can start working on those stories and beliefs.

A Spiritual Lens

If you don't think you deserve to be alive or feel worthy of life, remember, your spirit chose to be here. Your soul made a contract to be here, and maybe flirting with life and death is one of those struggles. What do you have to lose by staying here and finishing the story of your own life? There is so much beauty, depth, and love beneath the pain we feel. It's not a matter of if we find healing, but when.

Your life isn't some meaningless random occurrence or accident. Consider that every mistake, every chance encounter with a stranger, every hello, goodbye, choice, decision, drug, alcohol, late train, missed phone call, heartbeat of both of your parents led to the creation of you. If any detail was different or altered, as minuscule as showing up five minutes later to a party, you would not exist.

Now pull the camera lens back. That same notion exists for our parents, and their parents. You exist in a web of human connection that stretches out to infinity; you are part of the chain. Every interaction you have or don't have affects the web in some way; there's no denying it. You are a part of everything, connected to it all. There is no separate, no outside, no not belonging in the bigger sense.

To echo the first chapter, your spirit chose the exact body you're in, your family, your ancestors, this set of experiences, gifts, and challenges exactly because it knew the karma you have to work out. You are meant to be here. You are meant to alchemize pain into healing and awakening.

On a spiritual level, you could argue that if you're meant to kill yourself, you're going to do it. You could also argue that killing yourself creates more karma to be stuck in, and who knows what it will create in the next life. You might kill yourself in this life and be reincarnated as a slug. I don't know.

Some of the strongest and most vibrant people I've met have walked the line of suicide. They chose life and found beauty and healing after their darkness. I know you will too.

All Who Remain

Suicide is the ultimate "fuck you" to all the people who love you. You're not only skipping out on the restaurant bill, but you're making them pay the mortgage to the entire city block where that restaurant resides. Imagine the sixty or more years your parents, friends, and family will have to live without you. Every single day they will think about you and mourn you. If depression narratives are screaming, "No one will miss me. My life is meaningless," remember that those are just stories. Depression is a storytelling liar. There won't be a single day, hour, or minute that the people who love you won't think about you, miss you, and feel pain. I'm not writing this to make you feel guilty, but to remind you that the implications of suicide go far beyond just yourself.

I never met or knew Anthony Bourdain, but I still get overcome by grief when I see pictures of him. There are relationships with family members I never had because they gave into the pain and ended it. I'm angry that I never got to know who they were. I never got to spend time with them as an adult, never got to go over for dinner, hear their laugh, or discover their perspective on the world. It's unfair. It's painful and sad.

If you're going to kill yourself, I can't stop you. It's the one "freedom" anyone has at any moment, to end it all. It's really easy. Anyone can do it. It doesn't take a lot of skill, practice, a college degree, income, or knowledge. At any moment, any one of us can say, "Yeah, I'm done," and just leave. It's the path of least resistance.

It's harder to say, "I'm going to find meaning in this. I'm going to make this the best thing to ever happen to me. I'm going to get help for this pain and desperation I feel."

Failsafe

A friend of mine had a friend who was suicidal, and he told him about having a "failsafe." A failsafe is the idea that when you are lost in hopelessness and despair, what is the one last ditch effort you're willing to try that might offer relief? The bigger question is, when you're that low, what do you have to lose by trying this thing?

He recommended his friend go to Costa Rica or Peru and sit with Ayahuasca until something shifts.

As I've discussed throughout this book, I think getting in touch with the majestic and mystical aspects of life can help pull us down from the ledge. I have heard countless stories (including my own) of people being suicidal and Ayahuasca saving their life. It knocks you out of your head and can help you remember the divinity and sanctity of existence. Again, this is only one potential answer. Other failsafes could be checking into rehab, a monastery, or a mental health facility, trying MDMA or ketamine therapy, or going to a meditation retreat.

The reflection question for you is: What would your fallsafe be? When all hope is lost, what do you have to lose by trying this?

Just a Moment

In the last years of depression, when I was really hurting and the "kill yourself" voice was wreaking havoc daily, I came up with a rhyme that helped me. "One Day Soon But Not Now." It was the idea that if I wanted to kill myself, I'd push it to a later date. Just get through right now, just today. Postpone it until another day. I wrote a song with the title, and it actually worked to help me hold on long enough to find healing.

What it's like right now, it won't be this way forever. This moment will pass. Your pain is temporary. Just hang on. When I was in it, someone said, "It does and will get better." It made me want to punch them in the liver. If you feel that way, it's understandable. But it's true: It will get better.

Actions

My hope is that you'll use the tools, practices, and resources in this book so that you'll never entertain the idea of suicide. Working with beliefs and thoughts, you'll realize suicide is just another depression narrative. You can use mindfulness to come back to the present moment and always remember you are safe in your body. Modalities like therapy and plant medicine can help get to the root of our trauma. If you're feeling hopeless about a problem in your life, you can remember your true identity and where you derive worth. If you feel lost, you can come home to your inner divinity, spirituality, and faith.

Ways to Integrate This Chapter

- *Journal Prompt:* If you are feeling suicidal, spend time with the questions in this chapter and write on them. What is it that you actually want to die? The pain and suffering or yourself? Get specific. What is actually the problem here? Express the feelings and pain in creative ways.
- Call the Suicide Hotline at 800-273-8255 or simply dial 988.
- Tell someone. Speak it aloud. Find a friend or therapist you can speak to who can offer you a new perspective.
- Journal on ideas of a failsafe. Use, if needed.

Chapter Eleven:

CONSCIOUSNESS
A Mystical Conclusion

After enough medicine work, I have finally become the person that I've sort of loathed the most. I'm the guy that stops to touch trees to feel their energy. I get teary-eyed looking at birds. I'm that sort of granola-crunching nature-hippie that the old me would have glared at. I have profound micro-experiences that stop me in my tracks.

When I look at a strawberry, I see the vast and intricate design of complex universes. I see God. I marvel at how perfect they are, and I am floored by what kind of intelligence it took to make that. It nourishes us, is beautiful, and tastes good.

When I look at my hand, I see the same valleys and textures that make up the earth and desert planes. I marvel like a stoner looking at a Pop-Tart at the higher intelligence it took to create my hand and all the amazing things it can do. When I look at my father's hands, I see my ancestors stretched out from here to the beginning of time. I am just a moment, a part in all of this.

When I go outside, I see hummingbirds fly, tree leaves blowing in the wind, and nature as an eternal symphony that is always improvising but always in the perfect key. The path a bird takes is never the same. I witness a cloud and realize, at this moment, this cloud will never again be like it is right now. It's always changing, and I am no different. At this moment, my cells are dividing, and blood is moving, and I too am a witness and cocreator in this continual and eternal creation dance of the universe. Our bodies are mystical machines, taking care of breathing, digesting, and all of the other vastly complicated productions without a conscious thought.

Despite all of this wonder and awe, depression is still kind of an idiot because it thinks it knows what life is and how everything works. Depression is kind of like your uncle who shares flat-earther articles on Facebook. Depression is ignorant. It thinks it knows what existence is. It thinks this existence is boring or meaningless, that we are just meant to droll on day after day. It's dead wrong.

So far, we've looked at depression through a lot of lenses. I want to close this book by looking at depression as a matter of consciousness. When our consciousness is narrow, we are only able to focus on our suffering and depression, which can be hard to break out of. We are stuck in our pain, our suffering, with a limited view or hope or possibility of what can bring relief. When our consciousness is wide, we find freedom and embody unity, oneness, and love for all things.

Then comes the question, How can we raise consciousness? How do we get out of our own way and stop the suffering?

Experiences that raise consciousness—mystical experiences from psychedelics, meditation, yoga, music, or time in nature—can provide big healing and relief from depression by altering the way we see the world and reality. I tend to ask the plants whenever I need help.

The Plants Have Wisdom

I asked a shaman friend of mine how she would describe Ayahuasca. Her answer was intelligence. I would describe it as God.

For ceremonies, there are usually twenty to twenty-five people in a room drinking the medicine. The intelligence of this plant is so mega, the medicine is working with each person in a perfectly tailored and unique way, specifically catering to them, leading them to healing. It's astounding to look in a room and know that an entity is working with all these people at once in the exact way they need.

Ever since I drank my first cup of the medicine, my life has never been the same. The experiences I've had with plant medicine have made every single second of the ten years of depression worth it.

I've thought about it every single day. I'm thankful for every single day of my life because these experiences have been so profoundly healing. I've seen it radically change people's lives. I've seen it help people get sober and find peace. Here are the different ways I've seen that medicine can heal, based on my own experiences.

Root of Trauma

When I was first invited to sit with Ayahuasca, no one told me I had to get off antidepressants. I lost my shit. I'd been on antidepressants for six months, and it was the first six months in ten years I wasn't being obliterated by depression. Getting off of them felt like suicide.

My friend told me to speak to the shaman, and when I told him how afraid I was, he said something I couldn't argue with, "Antidepressants take care of the symptoms of your depression. Ayahuasca will get to the root of your depression." In my case, he was right.

While Western medicine treats symptoms, plant medicines get to the root. In Western medicine, we are dealing with human doctors and their limited knowledge about the brain. With plant medicine, we are dealing with a higher intelligence and divine consciousness that knows exactly how to help you in ways you could never imagine.

Plant medicine can go into your subconscious mind and find the root of whatever trauma you have and force you to face it head-on, which leads to healing. Often that root can be a forgotten subconscious memory, something no amount of talk therapy could bring up. People often say that one night of plant medicine is like ten years of therapy.

I'm not writing this to dismiss Western healing modalities. Antidepressants and Western medicine are both amazing tools that saved my life. Until they didn't. When it comes to Western medicine, zapping specific parts of your brain or taking pills for relief might only be part of the story. Sometimes a simple pill prescription can't take into account or doesn't resolve the existential despair or deep issues or trauma that a person is in. It can give them room to start functioning properly and do the work, which will lead to other healing.

Sometimes you just need a hug from the universe and a reminder that everything is ok, which plant medicine can give you.

Rewrites

Plant medicine can help you rewrite past traumatic memories in a positive and compassionate light. It can help rewrite the stories and narratives of ourselves. I've spent a lot of time on the medicine rewriting a lot of music trauma that I wasn't even aware was affecting me.

One night during a ceremony, I relived every tour I went on with my band. At that point, I still harbored a lot of anger and pain for the people we worked with. The medicine showed me their pain, how it was like mine, and how they were doing the best they could with the tools they had. Rewrite and perspective shift, point-blank. I got the message. I was able to let go of the suffering I had held onto for years.

Reconnect with Source

For depression, the power of this medicine is that it can help you peek behind the veil of reality and connect you with the source of everything, which is love. The medicine can give you the gift of remembering where we came from and who we are. Obviously, words don't do this justice. It's an experience.

Sometimes we get caught in so much mental chatter of unworthiness and unloveable-ness, the medicine just blasts us in the face with divine light and reminds us of our true state of being: joy and love. We remember what's important and what isn't. That experience can sometimes be enough to knock the depression demons back. It offers us such a different view and perspective of our problems that they just fall away.

I'm getting into a territory to describe the ineffable. To put words to things that are limited by our human brains. The power of this medicine is a mystery, and it's the most mystical entity I've ever come across.

This is work. It's not always fun. It's not a bunch of kids doing drugs at a concert. It's intentional and devotional ceremonies led by a vetted shaman. Some of the experiences on medicine are bliss, and some are uncomfortable and terrifying. I argue that living a life without it, asleep at the wheel, is the most terrifying of all.

As I mentioned in the first chapter, it gave me an entirely new worldview and perspective. I also want to mention again, these realizations can be achieved without plant medicine. As I write this chapter, I hear the medicine guiding me, telling me what to do. The bigger reality that the medicine is hinting at is that this life is mystical as fuck.

Life Is Mystical

Life is mystical. The creation of our lives and the creation of the universe is the greatest mystery. We exist on this beautiful planet in the middle of a seemingly infinite galaxy. We have absolutely no idea who made us or where we come from and no clue what's behind the curtains of existence.

Life is the greatest mystery and adventure of all time, followed by death, quite possibly the most exciting and biggest unknown any of us experience. We have no idea what happens next, and thank God.

Do you realize the magnitude of your being consciousness embodied? You are a soul in flesh! When we're depressed, we have a hard time seeing, cherishing, or understanding any of this. We are too busy with our own suffering.

This is why it's important to reach for the mystical. Open up your aperture, lean into the mysteries.

Just the fact that you are here, breathing and alive, reading this book with eyes—whose design and intelligence are as vast as the universe—is the biggest miracle ever. We are here, as humans, having this shared experience together. Just the fact that we exist is a big deal and enough to celebrate daily.

There is a sacredness to the reality that you have a heart that is beating right now. That you were born. That you have the power to create life. That you have the ability to feel things and experience the gambit of human emotions.

Society doesn't tend to place a whole lot of emphasis on any of this and instead places our worth on social following and bank account balances.

But you are a huge deal just because you exist, with a big beautiful life to live. I'm not saying this in a self-help bullshitty way, but in a genuine and mind-blowing way.

When we reach for the mystical and tap into the mysteries of life, which plant medicine or being astounded by nature can do, it opens up the aperture of our consciousness and can lessen our depression. When was the last time you had your breath taken away by something natural? When we realize we are an integral part of the creation of the boundless universe and we are infinite in nature, there is almost no room for depression.

I want to end the book as I started it: reminding you that depression is here to take you on an adventure. It's here to make you the best version of yourself you can be. I hope this book helped shift your perspective on it and changed your life in a positive way, and I hope one day you'll say, "Thank God for depression."

Ways to Integrate This Chapter

- Spend time with the mystical—read books or look into different forms of spirituality that might interest you.
- Spend time in nature—go to the ocean, lakes, and mountains; take hikes and walk in a park.
- Find micro and macro reasons to be awed by this world and this reality.
- If you feel called to do plant medicine, please do it safely, do your research, and consult your therapist, doctor, and mental health physicians.

ACKNOWLEDGMENTS

Mom and Dad: I love you so much. Thank you for blindly trusting me with this project and giving me the space, support, and spanakopita to create this. Thank you for always being my biggest champions. You are the best parents in the world.

Medicine: Thank you. Thank you. Thank you.

Joe Oleander: You saw a version and vision of me I couldn't see yet and didn't know was inside of me. You're a sage. Your insight, clarity, and wisdom were the seeds that planted the confidence for this book and my life path. Thank you for calling out the best version of me.

Jaime Fleres: I don't have words. This book wouldn't have happened without you. Your editing, your presence, and your encouragement made this book exponentially better.

Thank you for caring. Thank you for your attention and dedication. Thank you for encouraging me as a writer and human. You are an all-American badass and superstar. Thank God for you.

Tiffanie DeBartolo: You and your grace are the reason this book exists. You saved my life twice. I feel so blessed and lucky to know you. Thank you for reading the draft of this, for your masterful notes, and for proofing it.

Nicole Derseweh: Thank you for being you and walking this path with me in love, encouragement, and support. You are one of a kind and a gift to us all.

Dr. Courtnay Meletta and Luna: Thank you for being the mental health advisor for this book and for being such a supportive, beautiful, and wonderful friend.

Yia Yia Kiki and Hugh: Thank you for championing me and being the biggest inspiration and teachers in my life.

Sierra Smargon: You are an angel. Thank you for your help, support, and guidance over the past three years. You forever changed my life for the better, and I'm thankful for that.

Marcie Grambeau: I don't know where you came from or what you're made out of, but you swooped in and saved this book, the Indiegogo campaign, and my life in so many ways.

Thank You and I Love You

Elaine Nelson, Arwyn Moonrise, Kelly Baron, Jade Paris, Dina Martinka, Vika Semenova, Dana Marin, Lauren Hopper, Connie Cappos, Priti Gagneja, Sasha Nicole (Creature Divine), Summer Damra, Alexandra Cabri

Iván Chocrón, Kevin Garmin, (Thank you for keeping me sane and being a beacon of light during my Indiegogo campaign.) Juan Es Alzate Mejia, Universe Family, Claudio Cueni, ISTA, Daniel Heath, Daniel Robinson, (Thank you for bringing forth my light.) Dudley Michaels, Alvin Gill-Tapia, Ryan Scott Warren, Robert Price, Scott Schumaker

This book was entirely crowdfunded by raising $22,736 from 228 backers in a 30-day campaign in August 2022. As you hold this book, know it was brought forth by a loving community. I feel the spirit, love, and support of every person who donated to make this book happen. We rallied together to help heal and bring light to the collective. THANK YOU.

Thank You To All The Indiegogo Book Daddies and Book Mommies:

Barbara Kuhn, Beverly Van Wingderdan, Dave Hanacek, Livia Tortello, Courtnay Meletta, Joe Oleander, Yia Yia Kiki and Hugh Dyer, Nicolas Nayaert, Tina Khiani, Jaime Fleres, David Peterson, Jim House, Juan Gallegos, Daniel Gómez Seidel, Almar Hansen, Diane Kelly, Ashley Kummer, Alex Capobianco, Linda Allen, Frank Nicosia, Amanda Combs, Taylor Guman, Will Munslow, Dominic DiMauro, Anita Su, Dean Tompkins, Anna Bilic, Marcie MadeofLight, Joy Kinney, Tess Krieger-Carlisle, Joey Benenati, Gina Moon, Kate Weybret, Larry Siratt, Christopher Michael May, Brandon Stutzman, Michael Fish Herring, Filipa Marinho, Benjamin Forest, Kim Hagerty, Erich Riedl, Heather Aijian, Andrew Hackleman, Jayke Adams, Nancy, Vince and Mirra Tubiolo, Emilie Barnard, Robin Behrstock, Emily Zimmerman, David Johnson, Vivi Tziouvaras, Colin Gray, Apryl Kramer, Andrey Morozov, Chris Kastigar, Shellene Williams, Jade

Paris, Jeffrey Theimer, Bambi Barnum, Raven Waterfall, Mary Breen, Lauren Ginoberg, Bernadette Baocom, Ian Patrick Anderson, Dan Heath, Scott Schumaker, Arwyn Moonrise, Kathleen M Riggs, Alicia Diane Kotz, Myung Park, Michael P Nicolaides, Kevin German, Kara Pearson, Jason Souza, Meaghan Ryan, Glen Mercer, Erik Tyler, Giordi Frederick, Ashely & Christian Krueger, Lisa Phelps, Stan and Lori Nicolaides, Thorin Scott, Billy Watson, Jeff Clegg, Josef Kohn, Amy Grambeau, Pete Figliulo, Stella Cho, Rick Stollmeyer

Patrons From Patreon

I just want to specially and specifically thank all my Patrons from Patreon. Your support has given me the freedom and means to create music, art, and this book in a big way. THANK YOU.

Auramancer, Nicolas Nayacrt, Shelby Thomas, Steve Haynie, Andrew Hackleman, Claire Lewellen, Rob Kozacheson, Vladimira Doval, Meaghan Kalena Faulkenberry, Courtnay Meletta, Grace Leninger, Lorien Silverleaf, Matt Latham, Henrique Parizzi, Sascha Nicole, Cierra, David Stephens, Alexandra Melnikova, Erik Tyler, Lexi Decker, Arch, Brian Shea, Will Munslow, Alfredo Duenas, Jason Swan, Craig Murray

RECOMMENDED READING

Tao Te Ching—Stephen Mitchell version

When Things Fall Apart—Pema Chödrön

Be Love Now—Ram Dass

Light on Life—B.K.S. Iyengar

Bhagavag Gita—Stephen Mitchell version

Power of Intention—Wayne Dyer

Deep Work—Cal Newport

Universe Has Your Back—Gabby Bernstein

Jitterbug Perfume—Tom Robbins (This book has absolutely nothing to do with depression, but it will fill you with magic, awe, and wonder. It's my favorite fiction book of all time.)

ABOUT THE AUTHOR

Kyle Nicolaides is a top 10 Billboard songwriter and per-
former, leading the band Beware of Darkness for over a
decade, appearing on Conan, at the Reading and Leeds
Festival, garnering a top-five rock hit and 35 million streams
worldwide. He lives in Santa Barbara, CA. Find him taking
office hours at La Super Rica and Handlebar.

www.kylenicolaides.com
IG @kylenicolai

Made in USA - North Chelmsford, MA
1347467_9798987342206
12.20.2022 1337